£4.6

CW00500692

THE ANGELS KEEP THEIR ANCIENT PLACES

THE ANGELS KEEP THEIR ANCIENT PLACES

Reflections on Celtic Spirituality

Noel Dermot O'Donoghue

T&T CLARK
EDINBURGH & NEW YORK

T&T CLARK LTD
A Continuum imprint

59 George Street
Edinburgh EH2 2LQ
Scotland

www.tandtclark.co.uk

370 Lexington Avenue
New York 10017–6503
USA

www.continuumbooks.com

Copyright © T&T Clark Ltd, 2001

Extracts from Kathleen Raine, *Collected Poems 1935–1980* are reproduced with the permission of the Golgonooza Press, Ipswich.

All rights reserved. No part of this publication may be reproduced, stored in a retrieval system, or transmitted, in any form or by any means, electronic, mechanical, photocopying, recording or otherwise, without the prior permission of T&T Clark Ltd.

First published 2001

ISBN 0 567 08813 8

British Library Cataloguing-in-Publication Data
A catalogue record for this book is available from the British Library

Typeset by Waverley Typesetters, Galashiels
Printed and bound in Great Britain by MPG Books, Bodmin

CONTENTS

Publisher's Introduction vii

Part One: Introduction to Celtic Spirituality

1. A Spirituality of Place 3
2. The Bright Ring of the Day 17
3. The Imaginal World 25
4. The Celtic Imagination 31
5. The Angelic World 43
6. Three Aspects of Celtic Spirituality 51

Part Two: The Light of Other Days

7. Mystical Prayer in the *Carmina Gadelica* 71
8. The Lightener of the Stars 83
9. Nostalgia for Eden 91
10. The Mystery of Lamentation 97
11. The World of the Inner Self 107
12. Beyond the Concept of Heresy: The Case of Pelagius 115

Index 127

PUBLISHER'S INTRODUCTION

One of T&T Clark's best-loved and most distinguished authors, Noel Dermot O'Donoghue, is not one for the theology of dry abstraction. His writing is full of vivid imagery, warm reminiscence, keen intuition: it appeals to the imagination as well as the intelligence. His 'style' as an author is thus entirely appropriate as the medium for expressing the content of his thought, for it is poetic and evocative as well as precise. In this book he continues the exploration he began in *The Mountain Behind the Mountain* (T&T Clark, 1993) of certain aspects of the Celtic tradition, which is his own tradition, and especially what he calls 'the light of the imagination' as it is revealed in poetry, folklore and piety.

At the end of that earlier book, he referred to St. Paul's description of the 'resurrection body' in his first letter to the Corinthians. The new book takes off from that point. It is largely concerned with the 'imaginal' world and its relationship to reality and truth. The title is taken from Francis Thompson's poem, 'The Kingdom of God'. What Noel O'Donoghue is concerned to establish is the controversial idea that the writings of St. Paul and the gospel accounts of the Resurrection only make sense in relation to a 'lost category', a category of existence that has no place in a cosmos defined exclusively in terms of matter and spirit, the category of a 'physical incorruptible' world that in one sense is yet to come but in another sense *already exists.* This is the world of miracles, to which we have access through grace and sacrament and which we glimpse through the eyes of spiritual (as distinct from corporeal and intellectual) perception.

It is the world of the physical incorruptible that is evoked by poetry, music and song in the Celtic tradition, and in other traditions also. Creativity here shades into discovery, nostalgia into possession, nature into grace. We are speaking not of 'the imaginary' world constructed by the faculty of fancy, but of the true and supra-sensible world revealed by the 'wise imagination': an imagination purified and disciplined, ordered and healed by the grace of the Holy Spirit.

STRATFORD CALDECOTT
T&T Clark
January 2001

Part One

Introduction to Celtic Spirituality

1

A SPIRITUALITY OF PLACE

I

I begin this book of reflections with a kind of pilgrimage of the heart and the imagination to four Celtic places in the Isles of the North, two in the south of Ireland and two in the north of Scotland, places deeply imbued in very different ways by the Celtic soul, holy meeting-places of the transcendent divine mystery and the spirit of manwomanhood.

Let me begin by naming and locating these four places. You will find the two Irish places in the County or Kingdom of Kerry in the south-west of 'the green isle of Erin'. One is Inse Luachra, which lies in the northern reaches of the townland of Anneemore in the Parish of Glenflesk about ten miles to the east of Killarney town. Killarney is one of the world's great scenic centres where mountain, sea, lake and woodland combine to whisper and call and to shout 'Here is beauty', 'Rest here', 'Fill your spirit with reflections of heavenly visions'. Centuries ago the Norman and Saxon conquerors of Ireland took firm possession of this glorious land of lake and woodland, fertile green fields and hillsides, and bent the hardy natives to their will, building fine mansions to live in and lovely landscapes to drive in. The natives were left to find a bare sustenance among the mountains and rocky uplands and some of them fell back on the wilds of Claodagh and the slopes of the Pap mountains, sowing their meagre crops of potatoes and oats and barley along this green slope by a mountain stream where the rushes grew green and brown. This was/is

Inse Luachra, which is the Irish Gaelic for 'the uplands of the rushes'.

The other Irish holy place I want to call up from the depths of history is Skellig Michael, a rocky island rising out of the wildness of the Atlantic Ocean about eight miles off the Kerry coast, about sixty miles west of the two Paps and Inse Luachra, a place sanctified by a thousand years of prayer and the martyrdom of a saintly hermit carried off by the Vikings and made to die of thirst on the cruel shining sea.

Passing across the Irish Sea to Scotland, I shall ask you to make a pilgrimage to two places, both within the world of the Highlands and islands: one the island of Iona off the larger western island of Mull, south from Ardnamurchan, and the other a Highland kirk as deeply immersed in the Scottish Clearances as Inse Luachra was in the great Irish Famine.

All these places are sanctified by prayers and tears; all are embalmed in pathos – that pathos that carries its own inexpressible music that can be played only on the instrument of the human heart; all are veiled in that beauty that reveals itself as it hides itself: it will reveal itself more and more clearly as our vision becomes transformed into prayer salted by tears, held in its freshness by tears, tears sometimes distilled out of great bitterness, the long bitterness of the Irish Famine and the Scottish Clearances.

If we recall these places today and this sacredness of ancient and enduring sorrows, it is not in a spirit of triumphalism or in a spirit of revenge against the gross imperial powers of the past. Far from it. The fruits of empire have been sought as eagerly by the Celtic races as by the Anglo-Saxon or any other. No, it is to reach towards some of the eternal truths of the Christian gospel which shine gloriously across the centuries and yet have lain for centuries unregarded. It is to face a radical revaluation of values, looking primarily not to the dead past but to the future as it comes painfully and gloriously to life. It is to live with the living, flowing sanctities of the past illuminated by a memory-light that shines out of the future. I shall return to these points at the end. Now I must face forward into my main discourse, which is a kind of pilgrimage to the holy places of the Isles of the North that overtop the historic continent of Europe. I shall begin in Scotland.

II

The Isle of Mull lies off the west coast of Scotland across from the town of Oban. This is a few hours' run by road or rail from the cities of Glasgow to the south and Edinburgh to the east. Off the Isle of Mull is the Isle of Iona or Hycolmkill, a small island about six miles by three, nowadays a journey by ferry of not more than ten minutes from the nearest point of Mull. Today the boat docks easily and passengers can walk sedately down a ramp and look forward to staying in the restored abbey or one of two excellent hotels or take a chance on bed and breakfast accommodation; or they may choose to rough it in a tent. One way or another it is not an arduous pilgrimage once you get as far as Glasgow or Edinburgh, yet there is a sense of leaving the world behind and entering a special, even a holy, place as one leaves the Scottish mainland.

But it is not a difficult pilgrimage today nor is it expensive, unless one seeks and is willing to pay for the comfort of a good hotel. It was far different two centuries ago when two London literary men, one of them a Scottish laird, visited Iona in 1773. They could not step from dry boat to dry land but had to be carried, and though very well received by the islanders they nevertheless had to spend the night in a haybarn. Fortunately Samuel Johnson and James Boswell were both men of adventurous disposition and Boswell as a Scottish laird could, in those days, command service everywhere they went. Perhaps for once it was deserved, for Johnson, out of his store of wit and wisdom, had some very fine things to say about the experience.

These are all the more remarkable if one recalls that we are in the century of rational good sense and the sciences of hard measurable facts, so much so that Johnson went around making careful measurement of stones and buildings.

While Johnson observed the islands and the inhabitants, Boswell observed Johnson. Today we are interested in what Johnson had to say as he strode masterfully among the ruins of Iona. Here are a few sentences from a description that has rightly become celebrated.

> We were now treading that illustrious island, which was once the luminary of the Caledonian regions, whence savage clans and roving barbarians derived the benefits of knowledge, and the blessings of religion. To abstract the mind from all local emotion would be impossible, if it were endeavoured, and would be foolish, if it were possible. Whatever withdraws us from the power of our senses; whatever makes the past, the distant, or the future predominate over the present, advances us in the dignity of thinking beings. Far from me and from my friends, be such frigid philosophy as may conduct us indifferent and unmoved over any ground which has been dignified by wisdom, bravery, or virtue. That man is little to be envied, whose patriotism would not gain force upon the plain of Marathon, or whose piety would not grow warmer among the ruins of Iona.[1]

Clearly Johnson is seeing more than his physical eye sees. He is also making a distinction between two opposing philosophies of perception and he sharply disconnects himself and his friends from one of these philosophies, which he labels frigid. Yet it is quite obvious that his measuring-tape will not help him in the least in looking beyond the range of the frigid vision and the frigid philosophy of perception. But Johnson is a man

[1] Samuel Johnson and James Boswell, *A Journey to the Western Islands of Scotland* (Harmondsworth: Penguin, 1984), pp. 140–1.

of imagination and a poet as well as a philosophical observer. As a poet of the dawn of Romanticism, as a philosopher of the visionary kind, he sees more than the eye sees, more than in our own time the camera sees.

Here we are no longer in the cold mental world of measurement and hard fact but in the warm heart-world of *intimation.* This world has its own reality and its own limits, just as the world of scientific observation and technological measurement has its own reality and its own limits. It has its own spirit, too, its own 'angels' which may be destroying angels as well as consoling and transforming angels.

But let us return to Iona and its ceaseless clamour of wind and wave and the screams of the circling seabirds found all around the Scottish coast and the Irish coast as well. This unearthly commotion of the seabirds gives an extra-physical dimension to the world of human hearing, as the 'bright light-bridled waves' provide an added dimension to human seeing and the tang of the 'tangle o'er the isles' gives a further dimension of odour and 'the dearest freshness deep down things', felt by poets and by holy hermits at prayer. Seeing, hearing, smelling: there remain the great wide worlds of taste and touch. One wonders, did Johnson and Boswell, early romantics of the late eighteenth century, taste the wind and feel the touch of the machair under bare feet? Yet they surely belonged to the world of the shod generations far more firmly than did George McLeod, who discovered Iona for the twentieth century.

George Fielden McLeod was, like James Boswell, Johnson's friend and guide in his Scottish journey of 1773, a Scottish laird; he served with distinction in the First World War and became an out and out pacifist in the Second World War. He also became a Presbyterian minister and accepted a call to Govan in Glasgow, a very poor area sunk in unemployment. His answer to this was to lead the young men of his parish to Iona to set about restoring the ancient abbey on the island: he was one of the first to see that the worst evil of unemployment is not lack of money but lack of work as purposeful activity. He took the bold step of founding a community along Presbyterian lines connected with the Iona Abbey, as a result of which Iona has become once again, to use Johnson's phrase, 'the luminary of the Caledonian region'. To a Catholic observer the Iona experience is rather heavily scored by the Calvinist work ethic, but the connection with the ancient Celtic world of prayer has been kept alive by successive leaders of the community and wardens of the abbey and a lively collection of prayers from the Celtic tradition made by George McLeod himself is constantly in use. A recent husband and wife team of Celtic enthusiasts, Alison and Philip Newell, have accentuated this link with the ancient Celtic church.[2]

III

The island of Iona may be seen as a kind of gateway to Scotland from the west. It stands guard over the ancient territories of Dal Riada and the Pictish lands. It is a place of the guardian angels, of Michael especially, 'Michael the Victorious' as this great being was entitled and invoked in Skellig Michael and in St. Michael's Mount and Mont Saint Michel further south and west. The sacred places of the world of Celtic Christianity were all angel places. The poet of the hidden world all around us, Francis Thompson, he it was who spoke of the angels as keeping their ancient places.[3] For the present, as we stand among the holy

[2] See *Each Day and Each Night* (Glasgow: Wild Goose Publications, 1994).

[3] See *Selected Poems of Francis Thompson* (London: Methuen/Burns & Oates, 1907), p. 133. The stanza from which this line is taken is worth quoting in full. It goes:

> The angels keep their ancient places;
> Turn but a stone, and start a wing!
> 'Tis ye, 'tis your estrangèd faces,
> That miss the many-splendoured thing.

places of Iona where earth and heaven meet and the ancient remains are all around, I want to point to the symbol and the underlying reality around which the angels of light and the angels of darkness form an eternal congregation, the cross of Christ in its Celtic form of the haloed cross of the Resurrection.

Iona with its five high crosses is full of the symbolism of the cross of Christ and a small measure of imagination brings the angelic choirs before that inward eye which is part of our heritage as human beings. But this is not the reality, not even the historical reality, of the cross of Christ. For this we must travel eastward on our pilgrimage, ultimately, of course, very far east to Jerusalem and Golgotha, but these sacred places have been buried under layers of piety, unreality and triumphalism. No, we shall stay in Scotland and within the Celtic world. As we follow the way of the true cross, we shall visit the old Presbyterian church of Croick in the Highlands. This is our second place of pilgrimage in our visitation of the holy places of Celtic Christianity.

To find the small but historic church of Croick we travel north from the Cromarty Firth beyond Inverness on the A9 as far as the little town of Ardgay. At Ardgay we turn left off the main road along by the River Carron.

> It is a lonely countryside, its emptiness relieved only by one or two shooting lodges and sheep farms with here and there a clump of woodland and rhododendrons crowding behind sheltering walls. The road after two to three rough miles peters out at Croick twelve miles from Ardgay.[4]

It was within the walled burial area surrounding this little church that some of the victims of the infamous Scottish Clearances of the nineteenth century found a kind of crude shelter from the elements. They had been evicted from their

[4] I quote from an article by P. A. MacNab from the *Scots Magazine* of May 1963, i.e. prior to the renovations of 1982.

little crofts by order of the legal landlords of their holdings to make room for the Cheviot sheep seen as more profitable by the landlords, who found unscrupulous factors willing to carry out their wishes with cold and efficient cruelty: such was James Gillanders, factor to the Robertsons of Kindeace.

The only words that remain from the victims of the Clearances take us, whether by irony or design, in a different direction altogether. These words carefully scratched on the glass are 'Glen Calvie people, the wicked generation'. Let us suppose that the words are to be taken simply and penitentially. Not a prayer for vengeance but a prayer for forgiveness then, as these people face towards the wild ocean and a new land very far away. Nothing that we hear concerning these folk who took refuge here speaks of bitterness or revenge. Croick Church is a holy place not because it cries to heaven for vengeance, however true this may be, but because it cries to heaven for mercy and forgiveness.

And it calls to heaven out of the mouth of the blessed ones, the Christed ones, the afflicted of the cosmos, of the same cosmos that lies prone in the terrible grasp and all poisoning presence of the evil one. Only the Christ-prayer of the lamb who is innocent and who is slain can raise the wicked generation out of this total enslavement. Only the prayer of the innocent that take the guilt on themselves can open up the cosmos to the holy spirit of God.

Here, through this prayer of the innocent who assume the guilt of the guilty, here at Croick we have a truly holy place.

Jesus in his days amongst us was asked to respond to the much-talked-of calamities and acts of tyranny of the time. Instead of condemning the evil men such as Herod, instead of giving a facile explanation of the fall of a tower, he pointed to the whole human state, what has been called *la condition humaine*; he pointed straight at the evil will within us all and said: 'Unless you change your attitude radically you will all likewise perish' (cf. Luke 13.4).

It may seem strange to bring up these words in relation to the holy places of the ancient Celtic world. I do so after the fullest deliberation and in all seriousness. The Celtic way as it variously reaches us today through the heavy mists and tragic memories that cling to these holy places is a way of total trust in the divine presence and divine goodness – indeed, this presence and this goodness reveal themselves in a single profound intimation. It is this total trust and this triumphant survival by way of total trust that is the gift that now and always awaits the pilgrim who truly makes this pilgrimage to Iona of the high crosses, to Croick of the sacred windows, to Skellig of the angels, to Inse Luachra of the Great Hunger and the long, long road to the famine ships and the terror beyond the sea.

This total trust is easy to say, but it does not reach into the depths or the heights of its own reality unless it opens out beyond death and beyond the despair of hopeless days and endless nights towards the dawn that can only arise within the deepest, most entirely humble prayer of the human heart in that holy place that lies beyond all hope and all consolation. This is the intimation that awaits the Christian pilgrim who visits in truth these holy places of the spirit of the Celtic soul. I shall return to this intimation after we have completed our Celtic pilgrimage.

IV

We pass on now from the wild Highlands of Scotland to a famous island off the south-west of Ireland which is wilder still, wilder and lonelier and more terrifying. This is Skellig Michael off the mountainous wave-lashed coast of County Kerry, sixty miles west of Killarney of the lovely lakes and friendly hills, not far from the tourist route named the Ring of Kerry. You approach it through eight miles of wild Atlantic waters and there is little hope of setting foot on it during the winter months.

Here in the early middle ages there was a monastery of twelve monks and on the top southern peak a hermitage over 800 feet above the wild waters and the ceaseless cries of the seabirds and the clamorous winds.

The contemporary visitor who makes it as far as the ruins of the chapel and monastery is as besieged by questions as by the seabirds' cries. What kind of men were these ancient monks? How did they pass their days and their nights? Assuming they lived two to a cell, were they somehow bound together by special friendship (*anam-chairdeas* it was called . . .)? What kind of abbot bound these men together by his will and example? (One of them we know of was taken prisoner by the Vikings and died on the cruel sea.) How were these island monks connected with a supposed monastery at Ballinskelligs on the mainland? (Scholarship has still to explore all this and more.) Above all, how did they keep warm? (I do not mean bodily warmth, for they were tough, very tough, like explorers or seasoned soldiers. I mean warmth of spirit, the spark within, the mystical spark always or often receiving fire from beyond.) It is only those who have experienced something of this warmth, it seems to me, that can touch the life-springs of Christian, and especially Celtic Christian, monastic life. These men and, in less inaccessible places, these women carried the fuel for these soul-fires around with them in the form of Psalters and Bibles, and some of them spent a lifetime's love and care in illuminating these books by way of line and colour. These men and women lived within an ambience of prayer as the fish lived in the sea and the seabirds all around them lived in the wild air and the salt-spray of the sea all around. Of course this warmth could be found only on the far side of a life of heroic asceticism.

Besides the ruined monastery there is also, near the highest point, the ruins of an ancient hermitage probably dating back to the Culdee revival of the ninth century, about which a fascinating book has been written by two historians of art from the

University of California, at Berkeley.[5] The book is a remarkable account of an adventure in mountaineering and modern photography, and it completes Lavelle's standard (and indispensable) account of Skellig. This is how these pilgrims from a far country write about the 'feel' of the Skellig hermitage.

> To step out on the Spit (i.e. the vantage point above the hermitage) and look at the drifting clouds, the heaving ocean below, and the birds sailing above is to become deeply conscious of the primeval forces ruling the world. If one stands there on a summer evening as the sea-mist rolls in over Little Skellig, thoughts of the winter misery and hardships of life on the South Peak give way to wonder at the beauty of the scene. Something of the religious joy the hermit felt becomes clear, for surely the hermits of the South Peak shared the belief of another ninth-century anchorite who wrote:
>
> In Tuaim Invir I find
> No great houses such as mortals build,
> A hermitage that fits my mind
> With sun and moon and starlight filled. (p. 85)

I shall return to this vision and this way of perception. Now I wish to travel westward to the no less wild and ancient world of the breasts of Dana and the ruins of a famine village near where I first saw the light of day many years ago.

V

We are still in the Kingdom of Kerry, bounded on the west by Skellig Michael and the wild Atlantic Ocean, the *terminoi Atlantikoi* of the ancient Greeks. We have travelled inwards to the soft flowering beauties of the lakes of Killarney, to another

[5] See Walter Horn, Jenny White Marshall and Grellan D. Rourke, *The Forgotten Hermitage of Skellig Michael* (Berkeley: University of California Press, 1990). See also D. Lavelle, *Skellig: Island Outpost of Europe* (Dublin: O'Brien Press, 1976).

world, it seems, from the wild waters of Skellig Michael and the perpetual crashing of the waves and crying of the birds. Beyond Killarney to the east we come to another wild place, another sacred place named in pre-Christian times the two breasts (or Paps) of Anna or Dana, the fabled mother of a race of magicians called the *Tuatha de Danainn* who inhabited this place of hills and lakes and rivers long ago before the Milesians, the first Celtic settlers.

I grew to manhood among these hills of Dana and always and even now these hills are for me full of voices, full of presences; all of this was only one step away from some kind of commerce with the fairy-folk, the *leannann shee*, with a rather shy but ever present folk-consciousness all around me. This consciousness managed to cohabit with the angels and saints of the Christian story, with the demons also and the New Testament affirmation that the whole world lies prone in the power of the Adversary, the Poneros, the dark powers of Satan and Lucifer (1 John 5.19). This mountain range of Dana was, and still is, a place of spirits.

It is also at a more mundane level a place of streams and the sound of many waters. Just below the highest round of the Eastern Pap the Anneemore stream tumbles down and at one point the mountain becomes a kind of level valley. Here over a century ago was the famine village of Inse Luachra, a few small stone and mudwalled cabins with thatched roofs and a small field for potatoes. Nothing remains today but a few gable walls and the faint signs of cultivation each side of the mountain stream. Today nobody speaks of this famine village as such places were called, for they disappeared in the Great Famine of the 1840s as the old people died off largely through starvation and the young people left and went 'down the country' or managed to find their way on to a 'famine' ship bound for America or Canada.

There are many books relating to the Irish Famine of the 1840s, some of them of high academic quality, for the study of history has flourished in Irish universities, though the most popular book, *The Great Hunger*, was written by an Englishwoman, Cecil Woodham-Smith. New scholarly monographs appear from time to time, and 1995 has been regarded as a kind of anniversary of the first appearance of the potato blight in 1845. But the book that, it seems to me, gives the truest and most memorable account of the Great Famine is the novel by Liam O'Flaherty entitled *Famine*, first published in 1979 and still easily available in paperback.[6]

As I stand in the sacred site of the famine village of Inse Luachra I am contacted, even assailed, by the dead and by a life not past and gone but active in another light, a kind of inner transparency that, for all its 'lightness', somehow enters my imagination and takes it over, a world beyond time that is somehow awaiting me and awaiting us all. Memory and imagination together create a stage and the world within the world of the Celtic imagination somehow begins to occupy this stage. What a place for a young man or, maybe better, a young woman of talent to come and wait very quietly for the inner stage to be filled with characters and events and the holy incense of prayer. There is a rich and colourful world here for the fictional imagination. But what I sense behind it is not a fiction but another reality. This is not the kind of material, ultimately perishable, reality that men and women can control and which finally controls them. It is too gentle for that, too shy, a world of whispers blowing in the clean winds of the mountain blending with the ceaseless hurrying splash and spiralling of the waters, a world far more deeply interfused with divine presence, said Wordsworth,[7] poet of a world of intimations reaching back beyond childhood.

But it must be said firmly that this world flies in a kind of indignation from hard factuality and 'scientific' measurement.

[6] Liam O'Flaherty, *Famine* (Dublin: Wolfhound Press, 1994).
[7] See 'Tintern Abbey'.

The world of hard factuality that we control, and that has come to control us, has its own place and its own laws, even its own beauty – but it is not the world that we meet in these sacred places, where another reality beckons us onwards into the company of the spirits, of the angels and the good dead that await us and touch us at the horizons of pathos and prayer.

We do not seek these ancient places in a spirit of pride or imperialism, which would extinguish the light that gently suffuses their delicate whispering approach to us, but rather in the spirit of pilgrimage. We seek them in order to connect with the holiness of sacrifice that reaches towards the angels surrounding all altars everywhere and that meet us in the deep heart's core.[8]

[8] I must thank John Kelly of Carrigawanna, who has memories of the famine village of Inse Luachra; also Fr. Pat Moore of Gneeveguilla, who gave me the Berkeley book on Skellig. Finally, I must thank Mora and Alistair Munro who took me to see Croick Church on a dreich Highland day brightened by a car picnic above the Carron river.

2

THE BRIGHT RING OF THE DAY

I

I take the title of this chapter from an Irish song called 'Fáinne Gheal an Lae'. Now *Fáinne* is a ring, and *Fáinne Gheal* is a 'bright' or 'silver bright' ring, and *an lae* is 'of the day'. All in all, the phrase is a poetic way of naming the dawn in its first brightening in the east even before it begins to touch the hills and the plains and the sea with its lovely colours and becomes Homer's rosy-fingered dawn, *rododaktulon heos.* A new dawn, a new day, a day like all the days that have gone before, a day at once ancient and entirely new. Like first love, like the coming of the Holy Spirit of Love in that receptive prayer which alone deserves the name of mystical experience. It is this love and a new dawning of this love that I want to talk about in this presentation of Celtic spirituality.

I shall return to the imagery of dawn and daybreak and earth and sun in a moment, but first I want to anchor this introduction geographically and historically, and to do this I take a paragraph from a little book called *What Is Celtic Christianity?* by Elizabeth Culling:[9]

> Celtic here is understood as applying to the geographical regions of Ireland, Scotland, Wales, Cornwall, Britanny and the Isle of Man. By the end of the seventh century,

[9] Elizabeth Culling, *What Is Celtic Christianity?* (Nottingham: Grove Books, 1993), p. 3.

> however, the influence of the Celtic Church stretched from the Firth of Forth to the Thames estuary. The emphasis is on Ireland, since most of what can be said about Christianity here also applies to the other Celtic lands, and it is the most well-documented area. The time boundaries are from the mission of St Patrick in AD 432 to the coming of the Anglo-Normans to Ireland in 1169.

In accepting this definition or description I am leaving aside large questions such as, for instance, the extent and importance of Celtic France outside of Brittany, but it will do as far as our present approach is concerned. I am also leaving aside the complex question of the impact and aftermath of the Synod of Whitby in 664, in which the Celtic way as symbolised by the date of Easter was effectively outlawed by the central authority at Rome, though it seems to have resisted this centralisation for many centuries after this fateful day.

II

Over the centuries since the Synod of Whitby the great church centred on Rome has survived and flourished and spread to the ends of the earth. Yet the authority of the centre has been challenged – first by Orthodoxy in the East and later by Protestantism in the West, damaged most of all perhaps by the worldliness and politicising of its own popes and prelates. It has been shaken and challenged not only by Orthodoxy and Protestantism but also by various movements of the mind and spirit such as the Renaissance and the Enlightenment, most recently by Communism and secular forms of Socialism.

Not only has the great church survived all this but men and women of vision and spiritual genius, of holiness and heroic sacrificial fervour, have come forward at all times and brought back the holy fire of the original gospel to whole generations.

Great theologians and philosophers have also arisen, people who not only carried on the original Christian vision from generation to generation but brought something new to enrich it. In our day, there is Karl Rahner, using existential philosophy to affirm a supernatural existential in every single person of goodwill, even those who have never encountered the good news of the Christian redemption. There is Hans Urs von Balthasar, seeing the Christian cross shining through all human culture under the sign of beauty, or Teilhard de Chardin with his vision of the whole physical universe in its three infinities of the infinitely great, the infinitely small and the infinitely complex, all united in the glory of the cosmic Christ holding the divine, the human and the cosmic natures in the one person . . .

And yet in spite of all this and much more, in spite of an ever-continuing spate of books old and new, in spite of the unfailing prestige of the great centres of theology and religious studies, a kind of weariness has weighed down Christian thinking in the second half of the twentieth century, even though new movements such as Process Theology and various forms of Liberation Theology have emerged to enliven our hearts and minds. This weariness, this void has been consistently expressed by the great poets of our time: Eliot, Yeats and the rest. They have longed for something primal, fresh and clean, naked as fire and air and earth and water, innocent as man and woman in the garden of the holy forces of generation and growth and adoration, the first lightening of a new day in the east, the first pulsing all around us of 'the bright ring of the day'.

Once before such a dawning has come, followed by bright day and full noon and the shades of evening. Out of the Northern Isles it has come, the Christian good news renewed, emerging from the mists and spray and the cold winds and icebound solitudes of the north. So it was that Europe arose from those monasteries and hermitages that grew up around the courts and fortified palaces of the so-called dark ages and blossomed into the medieval schools and the high Scholasticism of the thirteenth and fourteenth centuries. The mighty achievement of medieval Christendom reaching onwards into the scientific and industrial revolutions of our modern and contemporary world – that is, Europe and the ways of European science and technology (Scotland must be named here) – so much of this in its restless and irresistible energy has come from the Isles of the North.

Today these technological and imperial, world-conquering achievements are being radically and continuously questioned and many people are looking for a new dawn over northern waters. Not from those energies that went forth to conquer the earth and build great cities but from that energy that looked within and upwards towards the Source, towards the God of creation, the God of the days and the seasons, the God of the holy places, the God of the heavenly hosts, of 'the mountain behind the mountain', the God who dwells in the deep places of the heart, ever ancient and ever new.

III

This ancient world, as it begins gradually to appear in a new dawning of a new day, breathes forth, whispers to us one word, a key word, a word known from the beginning but long forgotten, a word that has died the death of a thousand sophistications as the mind – the rationalising, cold, crystalline mind – took over from the heart and the deep caverns of feeling. That one word is *prayer*, that humble, heroic, all-consuming prayer which sent men and women to desert places, to mountain places, to lost islands, to the company of the wild waves and the cries of seabirds at the world's end. That one word is prayer, but not that prayer which is merely a weekly or daily duty in the *saying* of prayers, even in the common chanting of prayers, much less in the multitude and repetition of prayers, but in what can only be called the spirit of prayer and the daily, nightly service of that spirit.

By the 'spirit of prayer' I do not mean merely a general atmosphere or attitude but something very definite, very real, not something physical and measurable like the supposedly hard facts of what is called science, which are no more than mere appearance. No, the spirit of prayer lives and moves in that mysterious inner locality where mortal man and mortal woman connect with the immortal, the truly real that is also the truly good, the really true, the Beautiful, the Holy. It is the divine something in each of us, the *theion ti* of Aristotle and the Greeks, by which alone man is more than the passing, changing world in which he/she lives and moves. It is by prayer and only by prayer that men and women reach into that which is highest in themselves and thus rise beyond their mortal selves into their immortal selves.

When we look at the ruins of a Celtic monastery, whether it be Iona or Clonmacnoise or Gougane Barra or Skellig Michael, we are forced to face the question, What were these men doing? This question arises not only within the Celtic world but in other Christian centres and indeed in centres outside the Christian world. For the question we ask of these men and women is and must be a human question. And if we are to find light and guidance from the Celtic past it must be light and guidance valid for all human beings everywhere.

So let us ask and ask, Why? Why? Why? Why did they come here to walk into deep, deep loneliness in these desert places? Why this terrible sacrifice of all the colour and glory of human life? Of comely and companionable woman? Of all the brightness and colour of cheerful day? Why?

> I ask and ask, but no-one ever tells me
> What place we go when I meet Gaelic music
> And we are left a little while alone.[10]

[10] Thus Jessica Powers, the great Carmelite poet of the twentieth century: 'Gaelic Music', in *Selected Poetry of Jessica Powers* (London: Sheed & Ward, 1991), p. 77.

It seems to me that the place to which we are taken by Gaelic music in its original purity and the place to which these ancient ascetics and virgins were called are one and the same place. It is the place of the Song of Songs; it is the place of the Song of Mary, the virgin Mother, of the Annunciation and the Mater Dolorosa; it is the place of that psalmody which was the 'Holy Work', the *Divinum Officium* of these men and women of long ago who sought the wilderness for prayer as Jesus himself did when he went out very early in the morning to desert places to pray (see Mark 1.35).

Now and then, here and there throughout Christian history men and women (or women and men, as in the Teresian Carmel) have heard and followed the call of Jesus-Emmanuel to prayer and solitude, to prayer in community in the glorious and crucifying *agapé* of human togetherness. Now and then, here and there: men and women, women and men, old and young, young and old hear the call deep within, hear the call, and follow it . . .

We seem to be looking at the past and the dead ruins of the past, as when we look back to the days of Jesus and his disciples as they walked the roads of Palestine long ago. But to look truly at the past in its full significance and meaning, in its dimensions of spirit (and the spirit of prayer) is to look not primarily to the past but to the future. It is in this light of the past shining out of the future that I want to look again at our ancient Gaelic–Celtic places, from Skellig Michael to Ellanee (the Isle of Ee), *Iona insula.*

IV

In these ancient holy places, some now long deserted, prayer has been valid and the past rises up to meet us. People endowed with religious imagination feel the force of it and have a kind of inner glimpse or intimation of what I call 'the mountain behind the mountain', borrowing a phrase from the poet Kathleen Raine. These places shine and speak to us through the waves of time that seem to hide them, but for a certain imaginal vision only reveal their undying beauty. I have written a whole book about this[11] which tries to show that in such experiences we are in touch with a region of reality that I name the *physical incorruptible*, a region not far from the region of the angels and the saints, which I will explore further in the chapters that follow.

Against this background, I want to look more closely at the world of Skellig Michael and try to understand the spirit in which for over a thousand years men went to live on that lonely island rock nine miles into the wild Atlantic off the granite cliffs of the far south-west of Ireland. What vision led them on? What inner perception filled their eyes and ears and their other senses of taste and touch in that strangest world of all which is the thousand odours of sea and sky and land and the mysterious memories awakened by wind and weather and the warm airs of summer?

In speaking thus I am passing from the world of the physical senses to the world of the 'spiritual' senses, from the world of observation and physical measurement to the world of intimation and unmeasurable and 'unprovable' spiritual experience. The two worlds must not be confused. It would be fatal to look for, or to claim to have, scientific proof of the kind that is measurable and repeatable for our intimations and private certainties. It would be no less fatal to replace exact measurement in operating an aeroplane or an automobile with a feeling or 'hunch' that all is well and that all will continue to be well. There is the materiality, the physicality that depends entirely on exact measurement, but the world of experience is more than materiality, and it is by that more – that divine something – that man is immortal spirit and that he is felt called to prayer and in some cases called to prayer as *the only thing that really matters*. More and more, a new

[11] Noel Dermot O'Donoghue, *The Mountain Behind the Mountain* (Edinburgh: T&T Clark, 1993).

generation, carefully trained to stay within the limits of materiality, measurement and ever more sophisticated *processes* of measurement, are finding that this is not enough, that a world of perfectly computerised robots cries out that men and women are not robots, not even totally rationalised robots. *I feel therefore I am*; a robot does not feel, does not *really* feel, and in a human sense a robot simply is not. Above all, a robot is not masculine, that is to say, totally related to the feminine in all its transrationality and fruitfulness. We are touching here on the mystical and on that call that brought men for a thousand years to the isolation and loneliness of Skellig Michael, the place of the spiritual people who protect and transform the fallen race of men and women who sit in the dark place of the Great Adversary in whose power the whole world lies prone, *keitai* (1 John 5.19). Only the divine man entering within it, facing and outfacing its terrors, could break that power, bringing the angelic hierarchies with him and the good dead – all the angels and saints. These men went to meet the Lord God of hosts in Skellig Michael. They went to meet, first and last, the only begotten Son of the Father who was truly 'the son of the loveliest Mary'. The woman herself was with them there, and they had left women behind only to find the true glory of the feminine. You cannot understand the fearsome asceticism of this place where there is no woman unless you understand that it was not a destruction of the glory that unites man and woman but rather a purification, an *epithalamion*. They brought with them that Song of Songs which can be sung only from the terrible depths of the dark night spoken of by the Psalmists and the Prophets, by John of Fontiveros and, in our day, by a certain John Moriarty as 'he warbles his native woodnotes wild' in the story of Big Mike, alone in the lonely sea.[12] But that must wait for another time and another place.

[12] John Moriarty, *Turtle Was Gone a Long Time* (Dublin: Lilliput Press, 1996), pp. 213–21.

3

THE IMAGINAL WORLD

I

We all know that we experience the world around us, including the world of our own bodies, by way of the five senses: seeing, hearing, smelling, tasting and touching. Each of these opens up its own special world and together they build up what is called the physical, material, everyday world. These simple observations have hidden within them many problems and mysteries, but I do not want to explore these questions here, merely note that we all know what is meant by the five senses and the organs which they open up to experience.

To grasp this is to *see* it, but not in the way that the eye *sees* colour. It is a question rather of seeing with the inner eye of the mind, and for most philosophers this inner eye of the mind has contact with a world apart from, but closely intertwined with, that of the senses: the world of reason, of intelligence, of thought, of understanding. It is within this world that I see justice and beauty and reality itself. I see them as ideas that seem to shine in on the mind and somehow never change. Nor indeed do they seem subject to change. Just and unjust decisions and situations come and go all over the face of the earth, but justice itself never changes, though there may be deep and divisive discussions as to what is just and where justice shines forth in this or that particular situation. So too with goodness and truth and beauty. If we take the material physical world as the only condition and touchstone of reality, then this intelligible world in all its forms falls away into unreality. This is the approach of traditional Anglo-Saxon empiricism and those whose mind-set is deeply conditioned by this approach will not easily, if at all, open up to what I am going to say about the imaginal world.

Plato, Aristotle, Descartes, Kant, Hegel, Heidegger and nearly all the great philosophers outside the Anglo-Saxon tradition accept the reality of an intelligible or spiritual world distinct from the material world. But even those who agree with them may find it difficult to find room for the imaginal world; a world normally unavailable to sense perception but nevertheless real and important, indeed perhaps of central importance if we are to span the divide and heal the split between the world of sense and the intelligible world.

What is meant by the imaginal world?[13] How define, describe or 'locate' it? In general it can be located *between* the world of the senses and the world of ideas and it has one of its main properties common to each. In common with the world of the senses, it has particularity or concreteness; in common with the world of the ideas, the intelligible world, it has incorruptibility

[13] The concept of the imaginal world can be found under various terminologies in some well-known writers such as C. G. Jung (*Memories, Dreams and Reflections*), Rudolf Steiner (*Occult Science*) and Mircea Eliade (*Myths, Dreams and Mysteries*). Outstanding among those who deal with the concept directly are the French writer on Sufi mysticism, Henri Corbin (*Spiritual Body and Celestial Earth*, Bollinger Series XCI, Princeton University Press, 1977); the Scottish writer, Robert Crookall (*Ecstasy: The Release of the Soul from the Body*, Mornadabad, India, 1973); the Jungian or post-Jungian American writer of Latvian origin, Roberts Avens (*Imaginal Body*, University Press of America, 1982); and G. R. S. Mead (*The Doctrine of the Subtle Body in Western Tradition*, London: Stuart & Watkins, 1967). Perhaps the most powerful testimony to the imaginal world is that given by a magazine called *Temenos*, first published in 1981 under the editorship (mainly) of Kathleen Raine, an English–Scottish poet who has published studies of William Blake and William Butler Yeats. The magazine has been relaunched as the journal of the Temenos Academy, with support from the Prince of Wales (see www.princes-foundation.org). I have of course written more about all of this in my previous book, *The Mountain Behind the Mountain*.

or permanence. This is why it is the world or realm of the *physical incorruptible*, and this is perhaps as near as we can come to a definition or an 'idea' of it.

Let us look more closely at this definition. The imaginal world is a 'realm' or 'region' or 'world', that is, it can be understood in relation to the concept of reality as composed of several 'realms' or 'regions' which together form the totality of human experience. It is a physical world, a world composed of matter and form, yet its materiality is of a more subtle and 'spiritual' nature than that of the physical things of common perception. The Greeks and medieval 'cosmologists' conceived of several kinds of matter or levels of materiality and could even speak of 'intelligible matter', and we need to recover some such conception in order to identify the imaginal world. Certain esoteric traditions speak of etheric and/or 'astral' forms of matter, and this seems to be another way of approaching the imaginal world.

But why is it called 'imaginal', and how does the imaginal differ from the imaginary, or the imaginational? Writers of fiction 'create' worlds of imagination and sometimes show a special skill in making these worlds seem real even when they are clearly imaginative constructs, as with Swift's Lilliput or Tolkien's Middle-Earth. How does the imaginal world differ from these *imaginary* worlds? The difference is that we know intellectually that fictional worlds are not really of the same or similar stuff and 'substance' as the worlds of either sense-experience or intellectual experience. They are creatures of the human imagination understood as a creative or projective faculty. This faculty has the power to build up its own world quite freely and without having to trouble about the ontological or reality question – it is concerned only with questions of coherence, consistency, verisimilitude. Essentially the fictional imagination is free to construct its own world and does not have to face any criterion of reality outside itself. An event or situation needs only to be real within the fictional world created by the author. It is true that such fiction can serve a moral, psychological or 'sapiential' function, but this can be served equally well, perhaps even better, by historical fact.

Both the fictional world and the imaginal world are accessible to imagination, but while the imagination creates the fictional or imaginary world for itself (and for those who wish to share the author's fancies), the imagination *discovers* or uncovers the imaginal world. It must be said, however, that the division between the imaginal (what imagination discovers) and the imaginary or fictional is by no means absolute. Many artists, especially in painting and music, are convinced that their work is a work of discovery as much as, perhaps more than, a work of creation. An artistic medium or matrix such as colour or sound has within itself, waiting to come out of concealment, a whole world of potentiality or virtuality, and the imagination of the artist is forever searching to find truth and beauty within this matrix. It was Aristotle who first saw that there is a principle of privation or restlessness within the physical world, so that the physical matrix is, as it were, calling out to the artist to be given new form and new radiance. Thus the poet whose medium is the spoken and written word feels a deep stirring of imagination within him. By this he reaches out towards the world of images made by words and signification, to express anew for his time and place a celebration of truth and beauty – especially as this rises into presence by the deepest experiences of pathos and poignancy, of joy and glory.

There is a sense, then, in which the arts of the imagination are *discovering*, in the case of every truly dedicated and consecrated artist, a new field of reality in which men and women can find a homeland from generation to generation. This is true no less of the arts of the intelligence, such as philosophy, theology and mysticism, than of the arts of the sensibility such as poetry, music, sculpture and architecture. A philosophical treatise without the glow of imagination tells only of the world of death and dissolution, no matter how sharply and clearly it describes and discusses its principles. If it is true that in the construction of these monuments to human thinking intelligence is king, yet imagination remains the queen. The two belong together, and only together can they generate noble and beautiful offspring.

II

Imagination is a free faculty; it is not bound to its object in the way that the vision of the outer eye is bound by what we look at, say a mountain or a tree; neither is it bound to its object in the way that the intellect is bound when we try to understand justice or humanity. But we must try to distinguish carefully between two kinds of freedom and two kinds of imagination. Imagination of the first kind, called by Coleridge *primary imagination*, may be compared to a dancer who knows the steps and patterns of a ballet so well that she is able to bring a whole art of interpretation to bear on the tradition in which she stands. The second, called by Coleridge *secondary imagination*, is like a child jumping up and down on its mother's knee. This latter is also called 'fancy', and though it is basic and important it will not concern us here. Rather am I concerned with that primary or active imagination that opens up to a world or worlds beyond the everyday witness of the senses, and even beyond or distinct from the ways of intellectual discourse and investigation. Intellectual discourse needs the support of proof or demonstration at every step and is indeed, in its own way, a sacred and honourable occupation. Active or primary imagination, however, while it stays within the dance and does not step wildly and wantonly outside of it, opens up the dance to a kind of ecstasy that is totally free, because it has mastered the rules and rigidity of its tradition. In this case it is often said that the dancer feels the dance and feels taken into the dance. (That has been the magic of Torvill and Dean in their great ice-skating performances, to take a modern example.)

This active or primary imagination involves a high degree of attention and exactitude at the level of both understanding and performance, and it is only thus that the inner imaginal world reveals itself.

There is a vision of the world of nature which we find in poets such as Wordsworth, Shelley, Tennyson and Hopkins which is relevant here. Hopkins believed that when he looked intensely at a flower, for example, there was/is a real sense in which the flower *looked back at him.* In other words, the flower appeared not simply as an object in ordinary sense perception, but caused the image in the eye to enter into its own world as a kind of sharing of vision, as if we seeing humans are also somehow *seen* by nature's own visionary powers. Indeed, the human sensorium or centre of perception is intimately part of this world of vision, so that a philosopher like Berkeley could claim that, for example, the yellowness of the yellow flower had its dwelling in me seeing the flower, meaning not that the flower disappears into my seeing but that the flower and I both occupy a world in which vision happens and in which I share, as the flower shares in its own way. I can, of course, insist on seeing the flower as an object, perhaps the object of the science of botany (and this may be necessary for man's stewardship of the earth); but in doing so I have cut off that part of the flower and that part of myself in which we sing and dance together in the glory of colour. It is by the active imagination that this glory is given its proper space and its proper radiance, so that, as in Wordsworth's 'Daffodils', an inward eye opens up to an inward world. This is not a world of mere passing fancy but of a strong, deep, contemplative vision of the world of nature. It is the imaginal world shining through the objective physical and releasing it from the chains of objectivity and human domination.

4

THE CELTIC IMAGINATION

I

Let me begin this chapter by quoting in full a short, simple and very powerful poem by Kathleen Raine. The setting of the poem is that part of the Scottish Highlands from which the poet's very imaginative mother came and to which the poet returns after passing through a contemporary scientific education as a student of botany at Cambridge University. The poem is entitled 'The Wilderness', and it is a kind of lament for the vanishing of a sense of the imaginal world of 'the mountain behind the mountain' (that phrase that I find so evocative).

> I came too late to the hills: they were swept bare
> Winters before I was born of song and story,
> Of spell or speech with power of oracle or invocation,
>
> The great ash long dead by a roofless house, its branches
> rotten,
> The voice of the crows an inarticulate cry,
> And from the wells and springs the holy water ebbed away.
>
> A child I ran in the wind on a withered moor
> Crying out after those great presences who were not there,
> Long lost in the forgetfulness of the forgotten.
>
> Only the archaic forms themselves could tell
> In sacred speech of hoodie on gray stone, or hawk in air,
> Of Eden where the lonely rowan bends over the dark pool.

Yet I have glimpsed the bright mountain behind the
mountain,
Knowledge under the leaves, tasted the bitter berries red,
Drunk water cold and clear from an inexhaustible hidden
fountain.[14]

There is not one mountain but many, not one world but many, and in 'The Elementals' Kathleen Raine talks of 'the world behind the world'.

But just behind, and through the thinnest surface,
Not uncreated light or deepest darkness,
But those abiding essences the rocks and hills and
mountains
Are to themselves, and not to human sense.[15]

'Not to human sense' as commonly understood, for in the tradition that Kathleen Raine is invoking and expressing there is a human sense that can and does open to 'the world behind the world', 'the bright mountain behind the mountain'. Perhaps we should distinguish three modes of observation: that of common observation, that of life and death, and, shining through both, the imaginal mode, available to the poetic or creative imagination within a tradition of being and seeing.

The mountain of common observation is that which I encounter through the sense of sight and the other senses. It comes into my field of perception as colour and dimension and shape and 'thereness', solid, unmistakeable, the very paradigm, it would seem, of the real, expressing with absolute force the reality of the real. Yet even a little reading of the philosophy of perception will put this massive reality in question. The blueness and the greenness are not 'out there', for blue and green and all those 'worlds of light' that we call colours are subjective

[14] K. Raine, *Collected Poems 1935–1980* (London: Allen & Unwin, 1981), p. 107.

[15] Raine, *Collected Poems*, p. 106.

experiences that do indeed refer to what is out there, yet even this outreach or reference or 'intentionality' is simply a deeper layer of my experience. I am in the world of appearances or phenomena, and in order to approach anything that can be called real I have to undertake the mighty task of building up a world of essences after the model of Plato in ancient times or Husserl in modern times.

I do not want to push this analysis any further here but only to make the point that what might be called the privileged position of the world of common observation is not by any means beyond question.

The mountain of life and death is in some ways continuous with the mountain of common observation. But common observation does not normally and immediately reveal the fact that the mountain is teeming with life ever-renewing itself by way of death. What is perhaps most relevant to the present enquiry, leading, as it tries to do, to an understanding of the imaginal 'mountain behind the mountain', is that the mountain of life and death is already partly or largely outwith, if not outside, the range of common observation. As I listen to the voices of the mountain I am listening to life and death, and what I hear can never be really seen. The cry of the hawk, of the mouse or lamb in the death-dealing grip of the hawk, the song of the lark: none of this can be seen with the eyes of the body, yet it can all be heard and in being heard can evoke the poetic vision of the human observer, as a thousand songs and poems testify.

At this point there is a parting of the ways between those who see and meet the mountain materially and those who see the mountain spiritually. Those who see the mountain materially will see it as a place for grazing cattle, for quarrying stones, for perhaps finding minerals such as copper, or even what are called precious metals such as silver or gold. Such people engage happily in the exploitation of the mountain and see it simply as a place of exploitation and human possessiveness.

On the other hand, those who see the mountain spiritually are constantly conscious of a presence or presences behind what they see and hear and touch, somehow interfused with the colours of dawn and sunset, somehow seeking communication through the voices of the winds and the voices of the many waters, through the touch of the air and the mosses and the peat fields underfoot, through the scent of broom and bog-myrtle, through the taste of clear bright water and wild strawberries.

All this is the world of imagination and can be dismissed as belonging to the world of fancy. But fancy is merely imagination awakening and beginning to express its freedom, like a baby kicking about. Active imagination in its maturity – primary imagination – has come to take its proper place between reason and sensibility as at once servant and master in the house of human experience, where 'manwomanhood' is the shepherd of reality. Such an imagination is in touch with the transcendent world of universal ideas, with truth, goodness and beauty on the one hand, and the deliverances of the five senses on the other; also with the whole mysterious world of memory and the light of memory. While fancy is easygoing and playful, active or primary imagination works always by way of heightened awareness and a kind of deep empathy with what comes into the human sensorium by way of the organs of the senses. It is through this deep awareness and attention that the imaginal world shows itself as real, as presence and presences within a particular tradition, such as the Celtic tradition to which Kathleen Raine belongs and to which Yeats, AE and even Wordsworth belonged, as we shall see.

II

Four regions of imaginal reality can be distinguished within the Celtic tradition:

1. The fairy world of the *leannann shee.*
2. The world of elemental presences.
3. The world of the living dead.
4. The world of the angels.

1. The presence of the *leannann shee* or fairy-folk is everywhere in Scottish and Irish folk-tales and also in a great part of Irish literature, outstandingly in William Butler Yeats and in the delicate, but less finely wrought, poetry of George William Russell, who called himself AE (short for aeon or 'ancient spirit'). Yeats was a very great poet, a great craftsman, and his early poetry had all – or at least most – to do with what he called 'the host of the air'. In one of the earliest poems, 'The Stolen Child', he creates the atmosphere of the popular consciousness of the fairy-folk who are calling a human child to come with them.

> Where the wave of moonlight glosses
> The dim grey sands with light,
> Far off by furthest Rosses
> We foot it all the night,
> Weaving olden dances,
> Mingling hands and mingling glances
> Till the moon has taken flight;
> To and fro we leap
> And chase the frothy bubbles,
> While the world is full of troubles
> And is anxious in its sleep.
> Come away, O human child!
> To the waters and the wild
> With a faery, hand in hand,
> For the world's more full of weeping than
> You can understand.

Here a great poet is using the imagined world of the fairies to express powerfully the pathos of human life, and we are left wondering how far Yeats really believed in the objective existence of this world. G. K. Chesterton, a truthful witness, assures us that Yeats *did* believe in the reality of the fairies (see *Autobiography*). It is certain that AE firmly believed in the reality of the fairy world and in the kind of vision that connected with it. For what might be called a scholarly examination of this world we have to go to the Oxford doctoral dissertation of W. Y. Evans-Wentz, published under the title *The Fairy-faith in Celtic Countries* and reprinted, with a foreword by Kathleen Raine, some years ago.[16] Kathleen Raine has some sharp and pertinent criticisms to make of Evans-Wentz's book, but nevertheless it has not been superseded as a *general* account of Celtic folklore concerning the fairies. For further research one has to go to the folklore collections in various universities and scholarly 'proceedings' such as that of the Irish Folklore Commission based in Dublin.

But however much we study 'scholarly' works and collections, we usually find ourselves up against the 'scholarly' mind, which for all its honesty and thoroughness is not (as a rule) open to the reality of the imaginal world, and can only treat it as a folk phenomenon irrelevant to the spiritual world of modern man (the approach of the Temenos group is an exception).

2. In pre-Christian times, nature for the Celtic peoples was a place of spirits or gods such as Mananaan Mac Lir, the ruler of the seas, or Anna, the mother of the gods, after which the Paps of Dana (*Da Keek Anainn*) in south-west Ireland are named. As we have seen, Kathleen Raine refers to these presences as elementals and 'abiding essences'. One of our earliest Christian poems which calls on protection from various sources such as the Trinity, Christ and the angels has a stanza which calls on the elements and the spirits of the elements for protection:

[16] W. Y. Evans-Wentz, *The Fairy-faith in Celtic Countries* (London: Colin Smythe, 1977); first published in 1911.

For my shield this day I call:
Heaven's might,
Sun's brightness,
Moon's whiteness,
Fire's glory,
Lightning's swiftness,
Wind's wildness,
Ocean's depth,
Earth's solidity,
Rock's immobility.

Here the qualities of the elements are seen as presences contacted in and through the elements, presences which are so far alive and personal that they can be called or made present to answer to the need of the suppliant. Similarly, in this imaginal consciousness certain times and places were seen as auspicious or inauspicious, so that certain days of the week were seen as the right days for doing certain things, sowing seed, for instance, or setting out on a journey. The world of common day is seen as full of lines of significance that connect it with another world or other worlds. These connections are made by way of a long tradition, and living with them can become a way of prayer when it preserves a strong connection with the divine source, as in the Christian tradition of feast days and fast days and ember days.

3. The living dead are the people who have died and who are seen as in some sense still present with family and friends. This brings up the whole world of the uncanny, of ghosts and 'bogles', so widespread in the Celtic tradition. The evidence here is so complex that it is not at all easy to distinguish between the imaginal and the merely imaginary or fanciful. To understand the Celtic approach to the dead, it is best to turn from the field of imagination both primary and secondary to the field of memory, and especially to the ever-present memory of the

turning of the year in its seasonal cycle, wherein summer and autumn are forever dying into winter and winter is forever moving into the resurrection of spring and summer. The memory of the dead is forever becoming renewed and kept green with the greening of spring. The light of memory shines not from the dead past but from the living present and the eternal future within the present. I have tried to express this philosophical and mystical truth through songs in the Celtic tradition in an audio-tape named *The Roads of Long Ago.*[17] This sense of remembrance transformed into resurrection is present in all the many lamentations connected with mourning in the Celtic tradition, as in 'Aignish on the Machair' in the collection just mentioned.

In this tradition one does not try to make contact with the dead by any material means, if only because the dead are present in the world of prayer and the heart's remembrance. We do not call them to us; rather do we go towards them. They belong to a world of familiar mystery that is all around us, a pagan world in a sense, but a world wide open to the Christian hope of the awakening of the dead.

4. The angels are everywhere in the Celtic tradition, as we shall see in the next chapter, and they constantly serve to open up the divine dimension and to link the everyday world with that hidden world which is within and beyond it. A certain polytheistic angelology antedated Christianity, and this became easily and indeed eagerly transformed into the angelology of the Old and New Testaments.

It was and is because of its perception of the imaginal that Celtic Christian faith and practice had plenty of room for the angelic hierarchies. It was understood that the physical world of human perception is not only a corruptible world subject to death, but also a world of great light and beauty almost waiting

[17] Auldgate Records, Kirkliston, Edinburgh.

to show itself all around us, present with its own presences. The simple salutation used by the folk of my own boyhood said it all, for when one met a friend on the road one said: *God and Mary be with you both*, meaning, 'you and the guardian angel that is with you and that I somehow make present to me and to you by my salutation'.

So, too, in those exquisitely beautiful 'kindling' prayers to be found in the *Carmina Gadelica* of Alexander Carmichael, the holy angels are invoked as presences surrounding the hearth and the house. So too in the eighth-century 'Lorica' or 'Breastplate' of St. Patrick, so-called, one whole stanza is devoted to the invocation of the angelic hierarchies. So much has this tradition survived that I was no more than six or seven years of age on my own mountain in Kerry when I could rattle off, for anybody who cared to enquire, the names of all the nine angelic hierarchies: Cherubim, Seraphim, thrones; dominations, principalities, powers; virtues, archangels and angels. Did I see them? Do I see them? I leave you, my readers, to answer that question!

III

The light of memory shines not from out of the past but from out of the future . . . What do I mean by this? Take a song of remembrance of things past such 'Auld Lang Syne' or 'The Light of Other Days' (by Thomas Moore). 'Auld Lang Syne' is Lallans Scots for 'the time long ago' or 'the time past'. Now it is *I* looking back *now*, by way of my present power and store of memory, that can recover the times past. In Moore's song this present memory, this present light of memory which shines not only from out of my knowing mind but also from my feeling heart and so-called *fond memory*, is said by this loving light to 'bring the light of other days' with it and this now shines 'around me'. Now Moore, for all his sentimentality, was no mean craftsman in the use of words, and we can ask him what precisely he means by telling us that the (light of) memory coming to him in 'the stilly night' brings up another light which is 'the light of other days'. The objects illuminated by this (second) light are gone, blown away 'like leaves in wintry weather'. But it seems that somehow the light (of perception? of reflection? of love?) is not blown away but is *there* to be brought up, encountered, experienced, *and that with a new freshness.* This is the famous Proustian moment which can be triggered off by some quite trivial sense-experience in the present, as when Proust simply tasted a cake in a vacant moment and a whole lost world came up before his memory.

But does this 'light of other days' have its source in the past and its presence in the past, so that it is merely a part of the ordinary light of memory? Or does it rather have another source which is neither in the vanished past nor yet in the present memory? Surely 'the light of other days' is a light that does not in any way depend on one's days past, present or future? Surely the Proustian moment – and this is perhaps the core of the genius of that strange man – is a sudden irruption of a heavenly light and a heavenly presence that shows itself *within* the banality of the past as merely (chronologically) remembered. And this light is atemporal, outwith this temporal sequence of before and after, and so, as it were, shining from far off yet at the same time shining from near me and within me. Call it a light of memory, but it is by no means a light merely of recollection of the past as lived and blown away 'like leaves in wintry weather'.

Let us look now at 'Auld Lang Syne'. This is a Scottish folk-song which Burns refurbished in his own way and it has conquered the whole Anglophone world as what seems the song of remembrance. But here again the days of 'Auld Lang Syne' are not illuminated by the light of 'Auld Lang Syne' or by being in any real sense lived through again. What the song does, especially when sung with the feeling evoked by the words, is to call forth a kind of heart-light that is not far from the Proustian moment of transformed memory (transformed by the light from above), and that is turned right around from the past to the future mediated by that 'water of life' which we know as whisky, though it may be wine or indeed any shared drink. This, though it is sometimes darkened and distorted by that drunkenness in which the human disappears, partially or totally, is in its truth a sacramental moment and all the great liturgies are full of it. Indeed, every Christian knows that the last supper of Jesus was a symposium or drinking party in which the valediction was the passing around of a wine glass with the words: *Take and drink . . . and do this always in remembrance of me.*

So it is in the Eucharist especially that the ways and days of Jesus are brought into remembrance, not by a historical recall but by way of that light which shines on Calvary and the Resurrection from beyond time, and yet by way of the historical moment of the life, death, resurrection and ascension of Jesus. Through all this the Holy Spirit moves, bringing to remembrance all things that Jesus has said (John 14.26).

There is a sense in which all songs of remembrance are sacred songs, sacred because they touch a sacred spring within us, a light that softens and cleanses what was unloving and destructive in the past. It is perhaps because this light has an eternal source that it can *establish* human love, fleeting and vulnerable though it is, in a realm beyond all death and departure. This is the deepest feeling of songs like 'Danny Boy', 'The Boatman' and 'Molly Malone'. All this is deeply involved in the Celtic tradition, where the edge of sadness and grief opens up the world of renewal and resurrection.

It is only through an understanding of this that one can really connect with the liturgies of remembrance. They do indeed mourn the dead and evoke a whole river of tears, but this mourning should open up a kind of pathos that is truly homoeopathic. It heals the wounds of bereavement by touching these wounds in such a way that the funeral song of loss and departure opens up the hidden light within the memory of those same wounds: the heart of man and woman in mourning is touched by a strange balm which only certain kinds of music and ceremonial can convey.

5

THE ANGELIC WORLD

I

I want to begin my further reflection on the angels by looking at a book that very quickly became a world bestseller in 1994. The English translation published by Geoffrey Chapman runs to 691 pages. The copyright is held jointly by Geoffrey Chapman and the Libreria Editrice Vaticana.

The book is commended by a letter from Pope John Paul II which informs us that it is the work of a commission of twelve cardinals and bishops under the chairmanship of Cardinal Joseph Ratzinger.

I shall be glancing at what this, the *New Catechism of the Catholic Church*, has to say on angels, but before doing this I want to look at the logo which appears three times at the beginning of the book, on the cover, dustcover and title page. A note on p. iv carefully explains it:

> The design of the logo on the cover is taken from a Christian tombstone in the catacombs of Domitilla in Rome, which dates from the end of the third century A.D. This pastoral image, of pagan origin, was used by Christians to symbolize the rest and the happiness that the soul of the departed finds in eternal life.
>
> This image also suggests certain characteristic aspects of this Catechism: Christ, the Good Shepherd who leads and protects his faithful (the lamb) by his authority (the staff), draws them by the melodious symphony of the

> truth (the panpipes) and makes them lie down in the shade of the 'tree of life', his redeeming Cross which opens paradise.

So, somewhat unbelievably, the pipes of Pan symbolically play in the 2000-year-old catechesis of the Catholic Church. This is of course the great church of the great Western tradition that blended Hellenism, Judaism and Christianity. It is not the purified reform branch of that tradition represented by John Milton's great 'Ode on the Morning of Christ's Nativity', when Pan and all his companions vanish before the light of Christ. Rather does the great church find a place for Pan and the ancient gods, undemonised. For the ancient church, solidly based on Scripture and tradition, East and West, brought along its own Spirit-world. The ancient creeds see the creator as the maker of all things visible *and invisible*, for from the beginning the all-fathering, all-mothering source is Jahweh Sabaoth 'sitting above the Cherubim'. The hosts or armies of the Lord are the vast hierarchy of angels. This invisible world became part and parcel of the early eucharistic liturgies; it still holds its place in those prefaces or glory-prayers that introduce the central, most sacred, words and actions of the eucharistic liturgy: *et ideo cum angelis et archangelis*. So true is this that the celebrant who has pondered on the words and gestures he uses feels closely in touch with, indeed part of, this invisible world. The citizens of this world are all around, part of the congregation.

It is no wonder then that the mystics and theologians who serve this vision have much to say about this world, and I want to go on to look at what they say – or rather what some of the most typical and eloquent of them have to say. I choose two of them as illustrations, one a man arguably the very greatest speculative theologian among them, and one a woman who shines with special brightness among the mystics who are at the burning heart of the church: Thomas Aquinas and Teresa of Avila.

II

Thomas belongs to the high tide of Scholasticism in the thirteenth century and to that flowering of the combined wisdom of Hellenism and Christianity, when for a time the light of reason and the light of faith seemed to shine together into the minds of men and women. Part of that light was a kind of companionship of intelligences in which man, opening to the heights of knowledge and contemplation, was no longer alone but found himself/herself surrounded by a great and glorious heavenly companionship. The existence of these companions was, it seemed to Thomas Aquinas, guaranteed by sacred Scripture, and the main task of the philosopher-theologian was to understand and explain the nature and activity of these beings and how they were related to men and women understood as composed of body and soul or body, soul and spirit.

In this as in most matters, Thomas Aquinas made up his mind almost from the beginning. The angels are purely spiritual beings without the least admixture of matter to give them visibility or presence in space and time, though they might be given the power by God, as Gabriel and Raphael were, to take on human form and act in the human world. Not everybody agreed with Thomas Aquinas on this, though he found large agreement with his brother Dominicans. For Aquinas, to the horror of his princely relatives, had become a mendicant friar, a pious beggar of the order of St. Dominic. The other great mendicant order was that of St. Francis and they, more heart-centred and more earth-centred, brought the angels down to earth and said that they were not pure spirits but an amalgam of spirit and a kind of incorruptible heavenly matter – *materia coelestis* or even *materia spiritualis*. The great names among these Franciscan contemporaries were Bonaventure and John Duns Scotus. (We must take care not to confuse Scotus Eriugena, the ninth-century Irishman, with John from Duns, the fourteenth-century Scotsman: it was only in the eleventh century that Scotus meant Scottish; before that it meant Irish or Hibernian.)

But one may ask: what does all this mean in any terms intelligible to us today? Briefly, it means that the Dominican thesis (if I may so call it, on the understanding that I am myself in most matters more than half a Dominican) puts a great distance between angels and manwomanhood or 'humanhood', since they do not share a material component, that is to say a zone of inner receptivity which is not far from the human zone or level of feeling and instinct. This is the level that Origen and Augustine, as well as the Augustinian tradition to which Franciscanism belongs, called the spiritual senses, *sensus spirituales*.

The spiritual senses must be distinguished not only from the five physical senses of seeing, hearing, smelling, tasting and touching, all of which operate through physical organs, but also from the internal senses, so-called, of imagination, memory and *sensus communis*, to which instinct is sometimes added. The spiritual senses, as I understand the matter, are potentially in everybody, but come to development only in those who focus long and deeply on the spiritual world of the *invisibilia* or *supersensibilia*, or who belong to a living tradition in which these powers are understood and accepted. In the tradition of Christian Aristotelianism, to which the great Aquinas belonged, pure intellection was wonderfully and richly developed, to the extent that not only the power of imagination but also the possibilities of the spiritual senses were almost cleared out of the way to produce the great wonder of the *Summa Theologiae* of Thomas, while leaving less exalted projects to others. It was a world of light, white and clear and radiant, a world in which clear observation and clear abstract ideas filled the whole mind with 'large draughts of intellectual day'. This last phrase, perfectly applicable to Thomas Aquinas, was nevertheless first used of that other great witness of the medieval vision of the angels on whom I want to call: Teresa of Avila from sixteenth-century Spain, the *Siglio de oro* that shines across the intervening centuries.

III

We now pass from the high abstractions and intellectual constructs of the great Aristotelian Dominican to the very personal, very warm experiences of a woman mystic who arose within one of the great flowerings of the Franciscan tradition, a world of the spiritual senses in which those who do not understand it are easily led to confuse spirit and matter, the inner heart and its inner fire, with the vanishing fervours of the inner and outer physical senses. So it is that the following narrative of Teresa's angelic encounter is usually misunderstood by those who do not have the categories to understand what is being described. Here is the passage, taken from Chapter 29 of the *Life* in the Carmelite translation.

> I saw close to me toward my left side an angel in bodily form. I don't usually see angels in bodily form except on rare occasions; *although many times angels appear to me*, but without my seeing them, as in the intellectual vision I spoke about before. This time, though, the Lord desired that I see the vision in the following way: the angel was not large but small; he was very beautiful, and his face was so aflame that he seemed to be one of those very sublime angels that appear to be *all afire*. They must belong to those they call the cherubim, for they didn't tell me their names. But I see clearly that in heaven there is so much difference between some angels and others and between these latter and still others that I wouldn't know how to explain it. I saw in his hands a large golden dart and at the end of the iron tip there appeared to be a little fire. It seemed to me this angel plunged the dart several times

> into my heart and that it reached deep within me. When he drew it out, I thought he was carrying off with him the deepest part of me; and he left me all on fire with great love of God. The pain was so great that it made me moan, and the sweetness this greatest pain caused me was so superabundant that there is no desire capable of taking it away; nor is the soul content with less than God. The pain is not bodily but spiritual, although the body doesn't fail to share some of it, and even a great deal.[18]

Teresa is speaking of something *given* to her, but not given in the usual way, in the way you are given to me as I address you. If I suddenly see an angel among you 'all afire' like Teresa's angel, I am not claiming any physical *thereness* for the angel in the ordinary measurable physical sense. Something has flashed upon my inward eye like Wordsworth's daffodils or Housman's 'blue, remembered hills'. There is here a visionary moment, triggered off indeed by memory, but opening out and opening up to the fringes of that visible–invisible world in which the angels dwell. That world is so close to us that we can touch it in our prayers and liturgies (though, alas, more and more we are losing this touch, as is clear from the newer Catholic eucharistic prayers).

Even the Spaniards, in her own day or later, did not understand Teresa's encounter with the cherubic angel any better than many people today. Her physical heart has been embalmed and the wound of the angel's piercing is shown to visitors. It is no wonder that the angels, who are for both Aquinas and Teresa very close to us, prefer to remain in hiding.

Nevertheless it is worth the labour of trying to connect with what Teresa is telling us. Two things we must keep in mind as

[18] *Collected Works of Teresa of Avila*, trans. K. Kavanaugh, OCD, and O. Rodriguez, OCD (Washington, DC: Institute of Carmelite Studies, 1976), vol. 1, p. 252.

we look more closely at the text. In the first place, Teresa was a mystic, therefore not only given totally to active prayer but also deeply experienced in that receptive or strictly mystical prayer in which the Divine Source and centre takes over and lives its own tremendous life within the soul: the human person as related to its deepest centre and transcendency. This means that we are dealing with a meeting of depths rather than surfaces or even faculties. Secondly, though Teresa had several Dominicans of outstanding quality of mind and heart among her friends and mentors, nevertheless her mystical awakening came from Franciscan sources, especially through a certain Francisco de Osuna, whose book on mystical prayer opened up the mystical region to Teresa.

Dominican contemplation lives by light and by the vast reaches of the mind; it has never lost touch with that marvellous text in Aristotle in which he tells us that the last end and highest good of man (and equally of woman, for Plato's Diotima is in the background) is the contemplation of Divine Truth. This, Christianised, was mystical prayer as the Dominican tradition understood it. For even if we are called above all else to the *love* of God, it is surely only as we *know* God that we can truly love God in God's own truth.

But the Franciscan way is to seek *nothing*, to walk in total poverty. Aided by a Franciscan, Fray Peter of Alcantara, Teresa insisted on founding her Carmelite convents in poverty. God will provide, and that which provides is God, unless that same God is giving us the gift of poverty unto death. Total receptivity then, total poverty – even intellectual poverty. It is into this infinity of indigence that the angel comes. Physically, the angel is 'small', for its greatness is not to be measured by physical dimensions but in other ways. Its greatness is in its nearness to the Source, and to the fiery furnace of the Source and its marvellous and terrible invitation into its heart-breaking beauty. The story of the spear and the piercing has been accused of having sexual overtones, as if this were somehow criminal or surreptitious, but what it rather does is to give woman's *eros* its authentic glory and divinity. The angel is 'all afire' as the eunuch of the Kingdom, bringing back the holy fire of creative love to its Source, and thus renewing the Source in the possession of a new Eden. Perhaps we are going beyond our depths here, but some such depths lie behind Teresa's simple words.

IV

The high intellectualism of the medieval schools, represented with such clarity and power by Aquinas, and the high mysticism of the great nunneries and monasteries, rediscovered in her own day by Teresa of Avila, combine to give us glimpses of the heights and depths, the light and fire of Christian angelology. It has lasted as a central theme with various vicissitudes for nearly two thousand years, ever since the angel of the Lord appeared to Mary, and angels comforted Jesus in his agony and announced his Resurrection and his second coming. It is present, albeit as a very minor theme, in the Catholic *Catechism.* It has percolated deep into popular piety and folklore, so that, for example, the plays of Shakespeare are full of angelic presences: Hamlet calls on angels and ministers of grace to defend him, and Laertes invokes the ancient concept of ministering angels. The poetic imagination is never far from the sphere or spheres of the *invisibilia*: one has only to think of Rilke or Francis Thompson.

But of course there is one Christian tradition in which the world of the angels seems to have entered naturally and deeply from the beginning. As I have already mentioned, even when I was a boy over sixty years ago the famous plural salutation to individuals was still used, to include the guardian angel: the angelic world was at once recognised as part of life.

6

THREE ASPECTS OF CELTIC SPIRITUALITY

A. THE ASCETICAL ASPECT

I

As I explore my theme in a complex mood of weariness and excitement, images, intimations, thoughts and memories – and half-rememberings – flow into my mind and heart, seeking light, seeking warmth, seeking life.

Since I am Irish I think first of some of the holy places of Ireland, places of prayer, places of sharp penance, places of pilgrimage. I think of Lough Derg in the north of Ireland, also called St. Patrick's Purgatory, and its ancient, monotonous, debilitating, interminable rounds and processions, a place forgotten by the church of Vatican II because it was long ago put aside, drowned in the muddy waters of controversy. I think of Gougane Barra and its stillness and plainness like the austere old oratory of San Damiano at Assisi.

All these and many others were places of prayer and fasting, places where the spirit overcame the needs of the body, even the legitimate and necessary needs of the body. At the end of the twentieth century these places, these holy places sanctified by prayer and penance, by vigils in the lonely nights in lonely places, are doubly deserted. There are, of course, people among them, young people and men and women in their prime who visit places like Skellig Michael or spend time in Iona or Holy Island or Lough Derg in Donegal. There are people who visit Findhorn or some New Age centre, who make a pilgrimage to Stonehenge or Glastonbury and do not much complain of the hardships involved, and there are not a few who vaguely feel that the hardships are somehow an essential part of the experience. But hardly anybody feels, as the ancient ascetics did, that the experience is essentially and from first to last ascetical, a penitential experience which is seen and undergone as central to the call of Christ to give up all things and follow after him by steep and sometimes intolerably narrow ways.

II

One has only to dip into any classic of Christian hagiographical literature, such as Butler's *Lives of the Saints*, to realise how deeply asceticism and ascetical practice have become central to, almost identified with, Christian perfection. This has become such a hagiographical commonplace that it is almost essential to find authentic accounts written by the holy person themselves in order to reach any truth about it at all. This is especially true of the saints of the Celtic church, where an almost superhuman asceticism tended to become the criterion and touchstone of sanctity. Even when we are fairly sure that the saint's own account has come down to us intact, we have to ask ourselves how central and how constant this or that ascetic practice was in the true story of the saint.

St. Patrick is a case in point. The legendary material connected with Patrick is full of stories of lifelong and superhuman asceticism. But when we look at the only authentic document we have, we find a single passage relating to one period in Patrick's life, a period, he tells us himself, which is long over and seems to belong in the world of the fervours and excesses of youth, what spiritual writers sometimes call 'first fervours'. Here is the passage in the Wright translation.

> But after I had come to Ireland I daily used to feed cattle, and I prayed frequently during the day; the love of God and the fear of Him increased more and more, and faith became stronger, and the spirit was stirred; so that in one day I said about a hundred prayers, and in the night nearly the same; so that I used even to remain in the woods and in the mountain; before daylight I used to rise to prayer, through snow, through frost, through rain, and felt no harm; nor was there any slothfulness in me, as I now perceive, because the spirit was then fervent within me.[19]

This is the story of a tough, healthy young man deeply in love. If it were a woman that he loved we should not at all wonder at it, knowing well that it was a temporary state which at best would change into something deeper, less fervent, more constant, or at worst 'fade away like the morning dew'. Those readers who *must* have a hagiographer's holy man will always ignore or pass lightly over that last sentence, which is one of the most piercingly and soberly true sentences in the whole *Confessio.* Patrick, like every ascetic who has grown into the mystical, sometimes looks back nostalgically to the heady days of pre-mystical fervours and 'first favours', *mercedes* Teresa of Avila would call them.

Patrick stands or kneels at the source of Irish asceticism and gives it a particular colour and ambience. In the first place, it is strongly elemental and nature-centred, an asceticism set in the open fields and woods and mountains, among the animals that it was his business to feed every day. Secondly, it is an asceticism of prayer, centred on constant, reiterated prayer. Prayer is a kind of blessed fever in the blood which awakens him regularly from sleep and has become woven into his daily chores of feeding his master's sheep and pigs. This ragged youth of the glowing

[19] Cf. N. D. O'Donoghue, *Aristocracy of Soul: Patrick of Ireland* (Delaware: Michael Glazier), p. 105.

countenance must have been loved by these creatures who had come to depend on him, and thus a long tradition was started among the holy men and women of Ireland, a tradition which passed over to Scotland when St. Columba and his men went to inhabit Iona in the century that followed. Of course, the tradition of prayer in desert places goes right back to Christian origins and beyond, to John the Baptist, to Elias, to Jesus of Nazareth himself who habitually went to lonely places to pray.

Thirdly, the prayer of Patrick did not arise from any negative, life-denying ascetical motives. Rather was it the other way round: the deeply ascetical style of life arose from the fire within and was the almost necessary externalisation of that fervour. It is through an understanding of that fire and that fervour in Patrick and in the tradition he founded that we shall try to approach the mystical current in Celtic spirituality.

But it is well to stay somewhat longer with the ascetical tradition and for this we need to look at the sixth- and seventh-century Irish Penitentials. I shall do this in terms of a book called *The Irish Penitentials* by a young Irish theologian, Hugh Connolly, who spent several years of postgraduate study in Maynooth College and the Roman Gregorian University examining a sheaf of texts, about twenty in all, which together form the corpus of the Irish Penitentials.[20] These are mostly somewhat dull and dreary lists of sins with hefty penances attached, which on the whole seem more suitable to monks and clerics than to the common people. They are all based on a simple principle of contrariety: fasting is the medicine for gluttony, meekness for anger and so on. This was not public but private penance, imposed by a confessor or soul-friend, a matter entirely for the penitent's conscience, a matter of the healing of the soul. In our day the strict rules and positive, realistic principles of growth which activate Alcoholics Anonymous, for

[20] Hugh Connolly, *The Irish Penitentials* (Dublin: Four Courts Press, 1995).

example, echo the spirit and practice of the ancient Irish Penitentials and carry the same kind of conditional authority: 'If I really will to be healed, thus I must act.' I have come to see a twist in myself, echoing and reflecting the twist in the cosmos spoken of in the Gospel of St. John (1.29; see also 1 John 5.19). Jesus has come as the sacrificial lamb to undo, to rectify, that twist in the cosmos and in all of us. What the Celtic monastic tradition says is that we are all called to cooperate in this world and in all these ascetical and penitential practices by which the body is 'chastised and brought under subjection' (1 Cor. 9.27), lest the monk in preaching to others himself becomes a castaway ('disqualified' is the word used by the RSV). We are here in the full flush of that cooperational theology which was largely rejected by the Reformation, as it had already been implicitly rejected by Augustine of Hippo in phrases such as *massa damnata*; this theology was totally unacceptable to Pelagius, and totally unacceptable to the composers of the Irish Penitentials. There is still a very central controversy to be explored here. It is but one of the possible flashpoints by which the placid skies of Celtic spirituality may come to be riven by lightning.

III

So let us look a little more closely at the Irish Penitentials. They were Welsh and Scottish as well as Irish, but they seem to have had their deepest origin in the East, in Origen and Evagrius Ponticus and especially in a man from the East who came to live in the West, a fifth-century monk and writer named John Cassian. It was from him that the famous list of eight capital sins originated. They present a rather terrifying portrait of a life or psyche totally twisted out of shape. They are: gluttony, fornication, avarice, anger, dejection, langour, vainglory and pride. The penitentials are mainly concerned with providing 'remedies by contraries' for each and all of these deformations.

Thus the vice of gluttony is met by a regime of fasting, vainglory by humility, anger by patience and meekness, and so on. The list for the most part is identical with the list of the seven deadly or capital sins named by St. Gregory: pride, covetousness, lust, anger, gluttony, envy and sloth.

In the practical application of the discipline of the Penitentials the place of the soul-friend or *anam-cara* was very important. It was the soul-friend who took the penitent through the vicissitudes of life and through the final vicissitude of death. Yet we know little about soul-friendship or *anam-chairdeas*, just as we know little about the personal relations of ascetics and virgins, though there are intriguing hints here and there of a close non-sexual relation between men and women. All or most of what must have been a vibrant and varied way of life lies buried in history, just as the great monasteries of Clonard and Clonmacnois lie buried or nearly buried under the mounds of earth, after lasting longer in time than centres like Maynooth or Oxford or Cambridge.

IV

Before going on to look at that mystical prayer in which the labour and earnest striving of the ascetic bear fruit, I want to look briefly at some of the holy places of the Celtic Christian asceticism. The Isles of the North – Ireland, Scotland, England, Wales and the rest – are full of holy places, places where angels seem to dwell, places that can call us back again and again. There is of course Lough Derg, a place, still much visited, of harsh, somewhat relentless penance and hardships, like nuts rocklike in hardness that yet carry a kernel of sweetness within. Lack of food and sleep make it a formidable experience, yet people go there again and again, ordinary people, butchers and bakers and candlestick makers, ordinary, everyday folk. They return to the starkly penitential island, led not by fear but following a strange, age-old sense of the rightness of sacrifice. One can 'do' Lough Derg at any time during the summer season, but it takes three full days on thin soup and three nights, two of them sleepless; when it all ends at noon on the third (or is it the fourth?) day you are starving and you can only think of bed and eternal rest . . .

Croagh Patrick in the west of Ireland is another penitential centre connected with St. Patrick. All this involves is a barefoot walk up a steep incline for over a thousand (or is it two thousand?) feet, with Mass at the top and the prospect of a no less painful descent to level ground. By comparison with this and with Lough Derg, a pilgrimage to Skellig Michael seems child's play, once you can get a boatman to navigate the eight miles of wild water that separate this mighty rock-island from the mainland. Twelve monks used to live there at one time. Skellig has about it an atmosphere that is hard to put into words, as if the elemental spirits of air, earth and water were combining to erupt into fire and flame. It is one of the three places within the wildness of these northern seas that are dedicated to that great archangel who is 'like unto God and who protects humans against the wiles and snares of the enemy'. We are in the world of the spiritual combat and of that war in high places of which St. Paul speaks, a struggle taken very seriously by the ancient Celtic Christians.

B. THE MYSTICAL ASPECT

I

Let me begin this section by drawing a clear distinction between the ascetical and the mystical. The ancient scholastics, who knew a great deal about logical method, realised that such distinctions were best made on a common ground which they called the *fundamentum divisionis* or *distinctionis.* Here the common ground is prayer, and it divides into ascetical prayer and mystical prayer or, more intelligibly, active prayer and receptive prayer.

In active prayer one is striving upwards towards the divine source and creator of our being and of all that is. We are striving to penetrate the fascinating and tremendous mystery, the world of the numinous which is usually most clear to the wondering eyes of the child. As the things of earth crowd in around us, and as we enter more and more deeply into the world of common day, we begin to lose this sense of mystery and wonder. This, rather than the discovery of sexuality (the two are of course connected), is the great trauma of adolescence. For those who retain or recover the wonder and mystery, it is as if something beckons us on from beyond the world of sense and sensuality, the world which, with all its allurements, must at all costs be overcome and transcended.

Herein is the dawn of ascetical prayer, something to be treated with great reverence even by those of us who have long since left this dawn behind. This dawn-time may be full of the colours of sunrise and the dawn chorus of awakening nature, a time of sudden moments of heightened awareness and a fire within such as Patrick found in his loneliness and humiliation as a slave-boy long ago. This is the time of first favours and heroic decisions, the time of the *athleta Christi* such as Patrick describes. It is a passing phase; it passes over into the active life in its heroic dimensions, or into a kind of commonplace laodicean mediocrity, or – and this is its proper destination – into the mystical; more exactly, into the ways of mystical prayer.

We are here at a crucial point in the journey towards spiritual greatness of soul, that greatness by which a new world is coming into being, the greatness of a St. Paul, a St. Ignatius, a Mother Julian, a St. Teresa, a Thérèse of Lisieux. Such people are not only strong and fiery, endowed with oceans of light and a new vision, but are also beings of total receptivity, total humility.

At this point the spiritual roads divide according to a deep hidden paradox: the strong, successful people march on with courage and foresight and the inner power of their ascetical energy; the weak, deeply stricken people stumble along into the valley of Gethsemane where prayer is no longer sayable, where all tracks and trails vanish, where all is storm and smother and pathless desert. This is the true desert, *an diseart*, in which mystical prayer comes as a very secret manna, unfelt, invisible, intangible, delicate and shy as an old Gaelic *suantree* or *goltree*. Men and women of mystical receptivity, from St. John and St. Paul onwards, have received this hidden manna and lived by it as they lived by the Living Bread which came down from heaven; but only one mystic among them all could write clearly about it out of the simplicity and humility of her heart. Once again, I am referring to Teresa de Capeda y Ahumada, who took the name Teresa of Jesus and lived in sixteenth-century Spain. She was supported by many great men, including the religious genius named John who with terrifying realism took the name John of the Cross (1542–91). These men persuaded Teresa to write an account of her prayer experiences, and she wrote the book of her *Life*, meaning her life of prayer, in which for the first time, and once and for all, mystical prayer (she called it supernatural prayer) is made to stand out clearly for all to see.

Teresa, who had an almost unique gift for simple and telling metaphors, sees the soul or psyche or inner self at prayer as a garden that above all else needs to be watered. By way of ordinary or ascetical prayer we tackle the work of watering the garden by means of buckets, pulleys and windlasses, irrigation canals – all activities that are hard and laborious and provide meagre and grudging fruitfulness. But then, in a blessed moment when all seems lost, or at least intolerably hard work, the blessed rain may come, first drop by drop, then in light showers, in heavy showers, finally in a total inundation. As I stand by the ruins of the ancient Celtic settlements, from mighty Clonmacnois by the great River Shannon to wind-tormented Skellig Michael rising a sheer eighty-eight feet out of the wild turbulence of the western coast fronting the wide Atlantic – as I stand by these ruins in rain or sunshine I seem to feel that ancient flowing and growing outside of time, outwith the terrible vicissitudes of history in which the dark spirits were to have their day and their sway throughout seven centuries of hopelessness and persecution (to human seeming). At the end of it all, the *Miserere* is still being intoned and faintly, very faintly, as the soft evening light takes over, the alleluias of the Resurrection.

II

Even the solid, down-to-earth Dr. Johnson was quite carried away by the Celtic ruins of Iona and defended himself vigorously against the charge of sentimentality. So it is well to pause here and stand up boldly for the glorious reality of those great mystics of long ago who have left some delicate veils of glory clinging to these ancient ruins that lie all over the Northern Isles.

When we look at these ruins we all feel something of the cold winds of a life devoted to prayer and penance in total austerity. This is good and perhaps *does* us good. But this is not the point, not the *real* point. This approach, true enough within its limits, quite misses the joy and glory that vibrated through this way of life. Some of these 'heaven-havens' may indeed have been blighted with *acedia* (the falling away of spiritual savour) and perhaps the angels mercifully brought this process to an end, but as true centres of mystical prayer these places were vibrant with life and energy, work and recreation, tears and laughter, with the joys of honest fasting and honest celebration, even (though this chapter has never been written) with the *hagion philema* and the holy converse of ascetics and virgins.

At the basis of all this was mystical prayer and receptivity, but this in turn was fuelled not by meditation or contemplation in any exact sense but by the Divine Office and generally by what is called vocal prayer. Here is a passage from Chapter 30 of

St. Teresa's *Way of Perfection* which marvellously illustrates the kind of prayer, at once vocal and mystical, which permeated and vibrated through the many spiritual centres of Celtic spirituality for six long centuries.

> I know a person who was never able to pray any way but vocally, and though she was tied to this form of prayer she experienced everything else. And if she didn't recite vocal prayer her mind wandered so much that she couldn't bear it. Would that our mental prayer were as good! She spent several hours reciting a certain number of Our Fathers, in memory of the times our Lord shed His blood, as well as a few other vocal prayers. Once she came to me very afflicted because she didn't know how to practise mental prayer nor could she contemplate; she could only pray vocally. I asked her how she was praying, and I saw that though she was tied to the Our Father she experienced pure contemplation and that the Lord was raising her up and joining her with Himself in union. And from her deeds it seemed truly that she was receiving such great favours, for she was living a very good life. So I praised the Lord and envied her for her vocal prayer.[21]

The whole marvellous prayer-life of the Celtic monastic centres and the folk culture which derived from it, as mediated by Alexander Carmichael and others, was centred on vocal mystical prayer of the kind so wonderfully expressed by Teresa of Avila in this paragraph on the seemingly useless prayer of an old nun who was truly a great mystic. That a whole ongoing tradition and way of life should have lived this way of prayer for over six hundred years, opens up for us a great glory with which we need to make living connections for the third Christian millennium.

[21] *Collected Works of Teresa of Avila*, trans. K. Kavanaugh, OCD, and O. Rodriguez, OCD (Washington, DC: Institute of Carmelite Studies, 1980), vol. 2, p. 152.

III

The passage from Teresa's *Way of Perfection* is enormously wise and shrewd, extremely clever, in fact. It is a subtle attack on all glamorous and successful mysticism. It provides the portrait of a woman – not a learned man but an unlearned woman, not a choir sister with enough education to chant the Divine Office in Latin but a mere lay sister working about the house and saying the Lord's Prayer as she scrubbed and assisted in the kitchen. She was an insignificant being but for anyone of true spiritual perception a light shone around her.

This whole marvellous constellation of ascetics and virgins could only shine from out of that Christian humility ('Learn of me,' said Jesus Emmanuel, 'for I am meek and humble of heart') which could let God's glory through. This humility had as its companions the other virtues or orientations, backed by a positive and aspiring asceticism, for the mystical could only flourish in a soil prepared by asceticism. This humility in a man like Columbanus could be bold and challenging in the face of princes and prelates because it was without that self-love in which fear is rooted. It could face that slow, terrible martyrdom of the Abbot of Skellig Michael whom the Vikings, the messengers of Satan, tortured to death on the open sea. Perhaps worst of all, it could face what Abbot Colman of Iona had to face as his whole way of life and that of his brethren was rubbished by a proud faction at the Synod of Whitby; *that* history, too, still remains to be written. The strength of a great asceticism upheld all these true followers of Christ in their various calvaries, as they followed their master into the hour of the powers of darkness.

This is merely an opening up of the subject of the mystical aspect of Celtic spirituality as it arose in the Isles of the North. Much, much more could be said, and no doubt will be said as we try to recover more of that glory and that vision. I have, I feel, sufficiently opened up the subject. Yet not quite. One thing more must be said if the subject is to be more truly opened up. It is that the Holy Book of Christians was central to this tradition.[22] It was read in Latin and some of these Celtic translations are still used by scholars in establishing the traditional Latin text of that book on which European civilisation most solidly rests. The Irish monks also tended to have a keen interest in the Greek originals of the New Testament, especially the ninth-century Irish missionaries such as Scotus Eriugena and Sedulius Scotus.

In Ireland and Scotland especially, the Celtic spirit was taken into a terrible crucible after the glory of the great missionary centuries which culminated in the great St. Malachy in the twelfth century. In the terrible depths of this crucible lay the Irish Famine and the Scottish Clearances. The work of Douglas Hyde in Ireland and Alexander Carmichael in Scotland shows how the spirit of prayer, in both its ascetical (active) and mystical (receptive) aspects, survived it all. The Holy Book and a feeling for the original languages (Latin, Greek and Hebrew) also survived in the Scottish classical academies, and through what are called the Hedge Schoolmasters of Ireland: Padraig Colum's poem, 'A Poor Scholar of the Forties', immortalises one such wandering scholar.[23] This tradition has continued until modern times, but alas, my generation is the last to be given that marvellous gift of being able to read Homer and Virgil and the Greek New Testament by the age of eighteen. In Scotland this classical tradition is dying out even in the four ancient universities. This, rather than the depredations of Vikings and Anglo-Saxons, spells the vanishing of Celtic spirituality.

[22] See M. McNamara, 'Celtic Scriptures: Text and Commentaries', in James P. Mackey (ed.), *An Introduction to Celtic Christianity* (Edinburgh: T&T Clark, 1989).

[23] See also Daniel Corkery, *The Hidden Ireland* (Dublin: Gill & Macmillan, 1975).

C. THE VISIONARY ASPECT

I

It is not difficult to draw a distinction between the ascetical and the mystical once we see that their *fundamentum divisionis* or basic common ground is prayer and that prayer may be active and even laborious, or receptive with that active receptivity of enjoying a drink or a kiss or the glow of sunshine or the enlivening winds and showers. Roland Walls of Roslin, in a very homely metaphor, speaks of puppy dog prayer like a dog scratching at the door and the pussycat prayer of a cat lying by the fire . . .

But it is not so easy to find a way of distinguishing the visionary aspect of prayer and putting it in its place in relation to ascetical or active prayer and receptive or mystical prayer, although the earlier chapters of this book should help us to do so.

Let me begin with the category of knowing. We open to the world around us by way of the five senses: seeing, hearing, smelling, tasting and touching. Beyond the sense world, yet somehow shining through it, there is the world of thought and those generalised images we call ideas. There is a kind of reality about the world of thought which is admitted by most people who have tried to understand it, but it has never been defined or described to the satisfaction of all philosophers, though most follow Plato in thinking that our general ideas such as justice and beauty have some kind of reality.

All this is reasonably clear, though it opens out on great mountain ranges of mystery. But it is not enough to take account of the visionary world of Celtic spirituality.

II

Here is a picture or snapshot from my own past. I am just twenty years of age and I have come home from Maynooth to my father's house for the summer break. It is Tuesday, which is 'butter day', that is, the day in which the cream produced from a week's milking is made into butter in our old-fashioned churn – a staff churn. My mother in her quiet capable way has everything ready for the churning; my father takes the churn-staff in his strong hands and all the adult members of the family take turns with the work of churning. Suddenly there is a shadow across the half-door and a neighbour comes in. My father or mother takes hold of the churn-staff and asks the neighbour to take it, which he does and strikes it two or three times; his business is probably with my father and the rest of us go on with the churning. Before he took the churn-staff, as he was coming in the door the neighbour said 'God bless the work' or '*Bail o dia ar an obair*', thus putting his energy into the work that was going on. It would never do to omit this blessing or the little ritual that accompanies it. For the work of men and women was seen as connected with inner worlds, spirit worlds which every human being was affirming or denying; the transformative process of buttermaking was deeply connected with the wider transformative processes of the earth within which angels worked for, and demons worked against, humankind. A dark antagonistic thought in the heart of a visitor could bring in the dark obstructive powers to which the world in some sense belongs. When the visitor said 'God bless the work' this was no empty formula, but the statement of a stance and the directing of an energy.

As I heard the cream from our much-loved little herd of seven cows being thumped rhythmically into butter – very special butter because it was deeply spiced with the herbs and clovers of the mountain – I was half-conscious of all this opening to inner worlds as it flowed around me but I put it away comfortably in a cupboard marked 'Folk beliefs and superstitions'. After all, I was a devoted student of philosophy and science. This should have enclosed me in the world of careful measurement and metaphysical certainties. There was no place in this world for the vague feelings and intimations of the hill-folk of the south-west of Ireland.

As time went on, however, I began not so much to change my mind as to open my mind to further possibilities. I found Butler's *Analogy* and Newman's *Grammar of Assent* helpful, though I could not agree with Newman that there is a faculty or 'sense' within us by which probabilities become converted into certainties. What I began to see was that certainty and the desire for absolutes understood absolutely were, on the whole, bad for human beings, and that we have in us another faculty by which truth can be received gently and tentatively as an ongoing relationship and courtship. This, I saw, is precious, but it is totally destroyed if I grasp it tightly and fiercely as a possession held fast against all that would question or add to it. This faculty or power I came to call the faculty of intimation, and to this belonged those beliefs and ceremonials according to which the mountain folk all around me lived their lives.

The order of intimation must be sharply and carefully distinguished from the order of scientific proof. The order of scientific proof is based ultimately on careful measurement, on processes of measurement, on careful and accurate units of measurement, centimetres, kilograms and the rest. If I ask an engineer to build me a motor car or an aeroplane it will not do if he assures me that he is following a strong intimation that the car will stay on the road or the aeroplane in the air. He must give me what the Americans wittily call hard-nosed facts.

What I began to see or feel or understand as I thought about my Celtic heritage and also about those narratives such as the Resurrection, the Ascension, the multiplication of the loaves and the rest, in which the Christ-event and the Christ mystery are based, is that I needed a different kind of epistemology or theory of knowledge to understand them. It was not just that these events and promises belonged to a mysterious inner faculty called faith, but rather that they belonged to an ordinary everyday faculty by which the people of the churn-staff and their everyday small rituals connected with their everyday environment and communicated with one another. It was out of this intimational sense that the visitor at our buttermaking took the churn-staff, that my father went out every year at Midsummer to light the fires of St. John's night (*Les feux de la St Jean*, as the French peasants of the Celtic Auvergne call them) and that people I have known, ordinary, sensible people, go out on Easter morning to see the sun dancing, as did, to quote Carmichael, 'old Barbara Macphie of Dreimsdale [who] saw this once, but only once, during her long life'.[24]

III

What I have been calling here the visionary aspect of Celtic spirituality is what this book and my earlier *The Mountain Behind the Mountain* have been mainly concerned with: the world of intimation, the imaginal, the physical incorruptible. As we have seen, this Celtic visionary world gives a central place to the angels of the Old and New Testaments and fills the Celtic imagination with light and gentle companionship, countering the dark, destructive legions of Satan that have flooded the world since those miraculous early centuries of the great monasteries and missionaries from the Isles of the North. But these visions will come again only if the ascetical and the mystical come to be renewed. Herein perhaps lie the seeds (as of a fire under the kindling) waiting to flame and shine forth again in the years ahead.

[24] See Carmichael's note in Vol. II of *Carmina Gadelica*, p. 274. The new English one-volume edition reprints most of Carmichael's notes but omits this quite crucial one.

Part Two

The Light of Other Days

7

MYSTICAL PRAYER IN THE *CARMINA GADELICA*

In the eighteenth and nineteenth centuries the ancient Gaelic language, containing the oldest vernacular literature in Europe, was marginalised and outlawed in the name of the unity and glory of empire and the common imperial tongue, a well-meaning programme that did indeed bring great riches with it – Shakespeare, Milton and the rest – but which involved the loss of that divine and angelic vision enshrined in the Irish, Gaelic and other Celtic languages.

In the nineteenth century it began to be clear that the Irish and Gaelic languages were dying and that a unique Christian vision was dying along with it, a vision of creation, of man-womanhood, a vision of Godmanhood at once totally earthed and full of that breath and breathing of the eternal trinitarian Spirit, a deep-felt realisation, in the everyday of human living, of the reality and sustaining presence of the angels that came and went in the pages of the Holy Book of Christians. With this return of the regions of *invisibilia*, the ancient Celtic gods and goddesses have returned: Mananaan Mac Lir and Lugh, who long ago gave his name to Lughnasa, the month we name after the deified Augustus, and also to Lyons, first named Lugdunum; and Dana the Goddess, who gave her name to my own native mountain of Keeka Danainn, the Breast of Dana, in the south-west of Ireland, where Dana became the Virgin Mary for our Christian forefathers. Within this region of the *invisibilia* there was room for Pan as Aengus Oge no less than Dana as the

Virgin Mary. All this vision, all this ancient wisdom was lying there over the centuries waiting to be discovered.

Thus it was that when Alexander Carmichael, an Edinburgh civil servant (a collector of taxes, no less), was given the Western Isles as his bailiwick, he awakened to the fact that all around him in these Western Isles an ancient culture and an ancient language full of wisdom and light were dying out. So when he was collecting taxes he also spent every moment he could spare collecting the precious jewels of an ancient culture that was vanishing for ever. 'The likes of us will never live again,' said Tomás O'Crohan from the Blasket Island in the south-west of Ireland. In his beloved Highlands and Western Isles Carmichael went on collecting from the old people, while the young folk thought he and they were mad, and now we have the six volumes of the *Carmina Gadelica.* Ireland has also produced many volumes of folklore and ancient prayers (such as Douglas Hyde's *Religious Songs of Connaught*) but nothing to compare with the *Carmina Gadelica* for purity and power. Yet what the Carmichael collection does is to give a kind of centre and earthedness to a way of life and a vision of the width and depth of creation that connects Ireland, Scotland and Wales as well as parts of England and France, a vision that, more than anything else in the whole world, Christendom needs to regain for the building up of a new world at a time when all the lights that have guided us over the past few hundred years have gradually grown dim and almost disappeared. In this new world the ancient lights are reappearing, and it is marvellously significant that the pipes of Pan should, however faintly, announce the new *Catechism* of Catholic Christians through the logo on its cover.

I

There are at least three ways in which a modern reader can relate to that marvellous and much-discussed collection of ancient

Scottish hymns and invocations known as the *Carmina Gadelica*.[25]

First, we can look at it from a more or less strictly antiquarian point of view, unveiling as far as we can the original Gaelic oral text behind Alexander Carmichael's translating and editing. In this approach, the less of Carmichael by way of addition or commentary the better; indeed, certain antiquarian scholars have been rather dismissive of the *Carmina* from this point of view. More careful study of what Carmichael did and did not do has led to a more balanced judgement, however.

Secondly, we can look at the *Carmina* from a traditionalist viewpoint, finding ourselves variously open to the Christian and even pre-Christian beliefs and attitudes enshrined in this great text and in other texts too. We have to take account of the very different social and economic structures revealed in the *Carmina*, especially because we for the most part live in a highly industrialised, highly mobile environment, and are the beneficiaries and also the victims of a highly secularised culture and education, in which there is a strong inbuilt criticism of the simple pieties and customs of the people of the *Carmina*. The world of nature and the non-human living kingdoms have lost those presences and enchantments which form a constant background in the lives of the people who shared their world with Alexander Carmichael. In spite of all this, human nature in its basic instincts, emotions, aspirations and relationships does not change, nor does nature change but rather resists human efforts to change it; and so there is much in us which connects with

[25] The *Carmina Gadelica*, collected in the Western Isles of Scotland from 1855 to 1899, has been published bilingually and with ample footnotes by Alexander Carmichael and his family throughout the twentieth century (1900 to 1971) in six large volumes. This chapter was originally a paper read as part of a Saturday school in the University of Edinburgh to commemorate the appearance of the English text and notes in a single-volume paperback from Floris Books in Edinburgh.

these ancient folk and which is sometimes deeply healed by this connection. This is especially true for the contemporary Celtic world and there is already much revival of the past under way and even well on the way in various Celtic lands.

The antiquarian scholars and the traditionalist historians together, albeit differently and sometimes in controversy, have done much to bring the Celtic past, including the past of the *Carmina*, into view and indeed have sometimes given it new life and presence in the modern world.

But I want to talk mainly about the *Carmina* from a third point of view, not unrelated to the other two yet asking its own special type of questions and making its own demands. For we can also look at the *Carmina* from a theological point of view, and we must be careful to give this approach its own focus and its own space, both in itself and in its relations with philosophy and religious study.

II

What do I mean by the theological approach to the *Carmina*? I am thinking of the *Carmina* in its English dress, ready to travel the world as it were, since in linguistic terms English is a passport to the whole world, the lingua franca that has in our time taken over from French because of the importance of the anglophone United States of America. This version of the *Carmina* is ready to travel all over the world and it takes a challenge along with it to all those who live by the great book of all Christians, the Holy Bible in its various versions. I may add that I am looking at this book here as it has been understood in what I call the great tradition within which the Judaeo-Christian 'revelation' and Hellenistic philosophy have flowed together. But it is the Holy Book, affirming divine intervention in human affairs in an old and new covenant or testament, that is the main focus of attention, and I want to begin by recalling the Opening

Lecture of the 1981–2 session of the Faculty of Divinity of the University of Edinburgh at New College. In this lecture I tried to situate the Bible in a strictly academic setting: like Lord Gifford of the Gifford Lectures I argued strongly for the importance of natural or philosophical theology, and I have stood for this even against the prevailing tide within my own church throughout my whole academic career. This attitude is not simply concerned with the preliminary question of the reasonableness of Christian faith; it means, more radically, that the light of revelation is always mediated by the light of philosophical reason and cannot claim any such thing as a leap of blind faith. This does not rule out mystery or the mystical, but rather tries to understand and elucidate the concept of mystery and the far horizons of the mystical. This is true also of what I call the imaginal world of 'the mountain behind the mountain', a world that is always present in a trans-phenomenal mode for the people of the *Carmina* as it was and to some extent still is for my own people of the mountains and glens of South Kerry in the south of Ireland.

Here and there among these mountains, as in the Highlands of Scotland, you will come on a mountain lake deep and dark in which the surrounding hills and the changing skies, as well as any human habitations of peasant or chieftain, are reflected. In my Opening Lecture I called this reflection 'something understood', using a phrase from George Herbert, and used it as an image of the marvellous reflecting depths of the Holy Book as it opens to the whole of human life in the whole range of its poetic and philosophical experience. If you bend over the depths of the Holy Book too closely you will see only your own face and your own ideas reflected in it. But if you stand back from it you will see something of universal human experience and human history at once interpreting the Holy Book and being interpreted by it

This, I feel, is especially true of the *Carmina Gadelica*, and a theological approach to the *Carmina* must take account of this.

Such an account helps us to understand the way of life, and the way of the life beyond life, of a certain Christian tradition, and it also helps us to understand the Holy Book in new ways, and above all to enter into parts of ourselves which have been neglected by traditional Christianity in its various forms.

III

The part of ourselves that, neglected by traditional Christianity East and West, finds itself accepted and raised up in the Christian understanding of itself and of our human selves in the *Carmina Gadelica* is that in us which is continuous with nature, celestial and terrestrial, and with the sights and sounds, especially the sounds, of the natural world. From this point of view it is well to focus on the very first hymn of Alexander Carmichael's collection and also, or rather first, on the footnote or headnote that Carmichael attached to it.

> Old people in the Isles sing this or some other short hymn before prayer. Sometimes the hymn and the prayer are intoned in low, tremulous, unmeasured cadences like the moving and moaning, the soughing and the sighing, of the ever-murmuring sea on their own wild shores.
>
> They generally retire to a closet, to an outhouse, to the lee of a knoll, or to the shelter of a dell, that they may not be seen nor heard of men. I have known men and women of eighty, ninety, and a hundred years of age continue the practice of their lives in going from one to two miles to the seashore to join their voices with the voicing of the waves and their praises with the praises of the ceaseless sea.

> I am bending my knee
> In the eye of the Father who created me,
> In the eye of the Son who purchased me,
> In the eye of the Spirit who cleansed me,
> In friendship and affection.

Through Thine own Anointed One, O God,
Bestow upon us fullness in our need,
    Love towards God,
    The affection of God,
    The smile of God,
    The wisdom of God,
    The grace of God,
    The fear of God,
    And the will of God
To do on the world of the Three,
As angels and saints
Do in heaven;
    Each shade and light,
    Each day and night,
    Each time in kindness,
    Give Thou us Thy Spirit.

For us who live at the end of the twentieth century, Carmichael is the evangelist or human witness of the way of life and the religious world of the *Carmina.* We know that he has come in for criticism from purists who take the strictly antiquarian approach, but from the theological point of view he emerges as an authentic witness whose own glowing vision enhances the vision of these people and shows it off to advantage. It is not from a strictly antiquarian stance, which will always look for proof positive and exactly measured description, that we may rightly read what he has to say and the hymn which he puts at the head of his collection. We must read it as it was written, according to a vision or intuition of heart as well as mind.

It is one thing, however, to allow and accept as honest and sincere the enthusiastic words of a witness; it is another to let one's own enthusiasm amplify or exaggerate what he has written. Here the theologian must recall that the prior allegiance is to truth in its proper measure. We must look carefully at what Carmichael says, and note in the first place that he is not talking of the Scottish islanders in general but only of the 'old people' and that, moreover, this very moving description of old age praying by the ageless sea only happens 'sometimes' and is expressed in fairly poetic terms in which figures such as alliteration, simile and onomatopoeia are freely used. What Carmichael says in his notes is generally embroidered in this way and we have to ask ourselves how far the embroidery enhances and how far it hides the truth of the situation.

However, we must also see the *Carmina* collection as a whole and consider certain themes, beliefs and practices as they come to be woven into the texture of the whole. That is one reason why it is important to have the whole collection in one book in English and why I hope that the whole collection will appear, perhaps in a companion volume, in the original Gaelic. In the case of our present invocational hymn, all that Carmichael says somewhat imaginatively in his headnote is amply justified by the way in which, both in religious and secular poetry, the human voice is seen as blending with the voices of the elements; this also happens in the poems of the Irish *Fiannaiocht* tradition dating from the early middle ages.

When we look at the worlds of the rune or hymn itself, we see that its first part is rather sheer and transcendent, moving upwards to the immanent Trinity and only looking at the earth in the last few lines. Yet here a question arises which, if we ask it insistently, changes the whole intention of the poem from transcendence to immanence. The question is: why is the earth (*Talamh*) spoken of as 'the world of the Three'? The 'Three' means the three persons of the Trinity and the earth as 'the world of the Trinity' is set over against 'heaven' as the place of the angels and saints. And now it seems that the 'bending of the knee' of the first line and the threefold eye of the Trinity must be equally seen as an involvement with created nature, that created nature of which I myself am a part. We come to see that the reference to Christ and the Incarnation is not additional to the invocation of the Trinity but that the 'Three' are invoked *through* the Incarnation. In fact, the prayer is not transcendent in its goal and intention but rather is deeply immanent and, as an invocation spoken or sung by human voices, is indeed meant to blend with the voices of the sea and the winds and the birds.

This prayer is very firmly situated on the earth and within the creative forces of the earth, but nevertheless it rises up to the heaven of the angels and saints, to the source of all reality. Yet what rises up is the body expressing itself in voice and gesture and as part of the voices and forms of nature, for even the lark in the sky is seen as a kind of presence of the Virgin Mary. A woman from the islands, Agnes More Mackenzie, who does not seem to have met Alexander Carmichael, made a burial song which expresses how this deep connection with nature brought comfort in death. It is called 'Aignish on the Machair' and can be found in *The Roads of Long Ago*, a tape by Ellen Wycherley.[26]

IV

In the world of the *Carmina* at its most authentically spiritual and authentically Christian – a Christianity mediated by nature at all levels – we are in the air and atmosphere of mystical prayer. I believe that mystical prayer is the highest, deepest, most demanding and most spiritually transformative of all human activities, and here I am in agreement not only with the Carmelite tradition, to which I belong, but also with Plato, the Aristotle of

[26] This is readily available from Cathedral Books, Dublin, as is also another tape by Ellen Wycherley called *St Patrick's Breastplate* which includes, as well as the Breastplate in a new presentation, several songs, in the Carmichael translation, from the *Carmina Gadelica.* All Auldgate tapes may be ordered direct from Auldgate Records, 3 Auldgate, Kirkliston, West Lothian, Scotland. Among the *Carmina Gadelica* hymns included in the tape entitled *St Patrick's Breastplate* is the beautiful and profound *Blessing of the Kindling.* This is marred by a bad misprint in the single-volume English text (No. 82, p. 93). For 'loveliest' in the second last line read 'lowliest'.

the chapter on contemplation in the *Nicomachean Ethics* (Book X, Ch. 7) and the great Plotinus and his Christian interpreters. But notice that I do not use the word 'mysticism' nor the word 'mystical' in any general sense. Rather do I speak carefully of a form of *prayer* and it is only within this context that I find that the word mystical has any exact philosophical, psychological and theological significance. When people speak of the mysticism of Jung or T. S. Eliot or of the ancient Druids or modern Pentecostals, I do not question their right to use this language, but I wish to insist that there is something very precious, very special, very transformative, very divine that is indeed something other than what is spoken of in current loose, vague denotations and connotations of the term.

What first drew me, over twenty years ago, to the *Carmina* was that in the midst of much that was merely religious or pious or even plain superstitious, I caught again and again the gleam of gold, the true heavenly gold of mystical prayer. The human being who has reached mystical prayer has for many years given the first and central place in life to prayer, as Jesus did, spending, we are told, long nights in prayer; as Patrick did long ago; as in various ways all the great holy ones have done all through the centuries, those holy ones who live quiet, simple lives and carry deep within their eyes the gentleness of God, the mercy of God and something of the wisdom of God.

This heavenly gold, this shining forth of God's countenance, this anointing of the spirit is something *given*, something *received*, by those who are ready to receive it. This readiness will normally involve long years of seeking, of purifying experiences, as those blockages which are in all of us are dealt with: the passions and arrogances of youth, the querulous selfishness of old age. Moreover, the seeking of God in prayer cannot be partial; it must be seen not only as the most important thing in life but as the whole of life. All this is the way of active prayer, a noble occupation even if one never gets beyond it. This is the royal road that leads on to mystical prayer, and those who reach it are truly 'realised', even though they will normally have to encounter times and situations of satanic darkness.

Mystical prayer is sometimes accompanied by visions, locutions and other extraordinary experiences and phenomena, but the two are essentially distinct; indeed, visions, etc. tend, on the whole, to come in the way of that deep, quiet flowing and anointing of the spirit that is the essence of mystical prayer, which is so delicate that it is sometimes almost completely hidden and unfelt. Yet as an ambience or presence it is unmistakeable.

It is a common fallacy that mystical prayer is confined to, or at least most naturally found in, convents and monasteries. In face of this greatest of all human experiences all are equal, men, women and children, but those who see it as simple and easily attainable miss the point completely. Its simplicity is the simplicity of total purity. It is indeed a holy childhood, but a childhood appropriated at a summit of experience where grace freely received leads the way. Mystical prayer must be distinguished from asceticism, yet it belongs most naturally to a simple, ascetical, unpretentious way of life such as radiates from the *Carmina Gadelica.*

There are young people in whom a deep innocence and joy is miraculously preserved; there are old people whose lives are bathed in mystical prayer: you may find one or two of them who have found a peaceful place in a city or country church or even a public library, or in a kind of daily routine. These are the great ones of the earth, the salt that keeps the human mass from total corruption, and sometimes, as in the Jewish Holocaust or the Irish Famine, they arise in a great *martyrion* of common witness. It was on such a group as this that Alexander Carmichael stumbled when he was sent to the Western Isles of Scotland as a government tax inspector. He felt a great fragrance around him and tried to make it available to all in the time to come. It is a delicate matter that such a fragrance can survive in other vessels than those in which it was first placed as a kind of priestly act by Carmichael himself. We are lucky that it became a sacred family heritage, so that the further volumes of the *Carmina* appeared and are still available.

8

THE LIGHTENER OF THE STARS

I

The poem or hymn entitled 'The Lightener of the Stars' will be found in the original Gaelic as given to Alexander Carmichael by an old woman of the Isle of Barra and in Carmichael's English translation of the Gaelic *Carmina Gadelica*.[27]

I have chosen this hymn as a way of entry into what is, as I see it, central and even special to the Celtic spiritual tradition, a tradition that goes back beyond the Reformation and also beyond the Synod of Whitby in the seventh century, a Catholic tradition that does not define itself negatively in opposition to the Reformation or positively in terms of a strongly centralised ultramontane Catholicism.

Nevertheless the hymn, however ancient it may be, was set down in writing only in the middle of the nineteenth century; and thus it represents a kind of living link with the far Christian past and with a vision that has almost disappeared from our modern world. This vision is related to a kind of light that is neither the light of the physical eyes nor yet the inner light of faith or intellectual understanding. Rather, it is a third kind of light which was at once the light *within* physical light and also the light that connected the physical world with the spiritual worlds that flow through it and rise beyond it.

[27] *Carmina Gadelica I*, pp. 44–5.

II

Here is the hymn, '*Sorchar nan Reul*', in Carmichael's translation:

Behold the Lightener of the stars
On the crests of the clouds,
And the choralists of the sky
Lauding Him.

Coming down with acclaim
From the Father above,
Harp and lyre of song
Sounding to Him.

Christ, Thou refuge of my love,
Why should not I raise Thy fame!
Angels and saints melodious
Singing to Thee.

Thou Son of the Mary of graces,
Of exceeding white purity of beauty,
Joy were it to me to be in the fields
Of Thy riches.

O Christ my beloved,
O Christ of the Holy Blood,
By day and by night
I praise Thee.

The word 'lightener' simply means 'the one who illuminates' or gives light. We have here a Christmas hymn in which the new-born Christ-child is bringing with him the light that gives their light to the bright shining stars, the true light not only of the minds of men and women but also of the physical stars in their visibility to human eyes. We can miss the point here if we situate ourselves within the world of metaphor, as if, with the poet Hopkins, we were to look up at the stars and see 'all the fire-folk' ranged above us. Hopkins is, in fine poetic vein, expressing his (and our) sense of awe and wonder at the manifold glory of God's creation against the background of a firm yet mystery-laden faith in the creator-God. One does not have to cease to admire Hopkins' opening of the windows of wonder in order to claim that *this* Christmas hymn, which emerges fresh and clear from the Celtic tradition, is not dealing in metaphors, but rather expresses a vision that belongs to the world of the spiritual senses such as we find in Origen and Augustine, and, in the general mystical tradition, relates especially to the anagogical interpretation of the Song of Songs. If I may rehearse this once more, this spiritual-sensible seeing is at once physical and, at the same time, incorruptible. It is by the exercise of this inner seeing that the Celtic tradition saw the Christ-light as the light *within* the light that comes to us from the sun and the stars. It is this light that is seen within the sun that dances at Easter.[28] It is seen by way of an inner vision that is deeply connected with prayer and faith. It is *given* to the inner eye of imagination, not projected but received, not contacted by *active* prayer, not at all constrained by one's own desires or deservings. It is strictly mystical, that is, it can be given and received only within a lifetime of total dedication to prayer. It is out of this inner perception of the light within the light that the hymn repeated by Fiona McDougal, the old woman of Barra, to Alexander Carmichael, and set down in writing for the first time, must have been composed.

III

The hymn '*Sorchar nan Reul*' came out of an inner seeing; it also came out of an inner hearing of 'the choralists of the sky' who are the angels, who are joined by the 'good dead', the saints, in the third stanza. These do not take away from the surpassing

[28] See *Carmina Gadelica II*, p. 274; also *The Mountain Behind the Mountain*, ch. 2.

divine glory of the true light that is coming straight 'from the Father above'; rather is it fitting that (as in St. Luke's Gospel) a multitude of the heavenly army should proclaim his coming and his glory. The angels are not the distant, entirely disembodied angels of the Thomist tradition but rather those Franciscan angels of Duns Scotus and Francisco de Osuna, angels composed of that *materia coelestis* by which they could connect closely with human hearing and human feeling, as in that 'transverberation' of Teresa which she carefully records for us in terms of felt personal experience in Chapter 29 of the *Life*. And so we have the shaper of our Christmas hymn connecting very personally with the angelic world, carrying harp and lyre as Teresa's angel carried a spear tipped with fire.

Of course in all this the human imagination is at work, an imagination coloured and heightened by prayer and habits of faith. We are not in the scientifically measurable, experimentally repeatable world of ordinary common 'public' perception, but it is in this measurable world that we must live and move if we are to dominate our environment, bring it into service and accurately control it. And we mix and confuse the world of measurable 'public' perception with our worlds of inner or spiritual perception at our own peril; that way madness lies. This is plain common sense, and nobody knows it better than did the men and women from whom Carmichael collected his hymns and invocations: the men who dug the hard grudging fields or ventured in their frail curraghs on the uncertain and merciless ocean, the women who milked their few cows and prepared the wool for the making of cloth. Men and women, they sang at their work; men and women, they were conscious of the 'presences' around them; but no people anywhere on 'the round globe of earth' were more conscious of the causality of things and the iron law that two and two make four and not five or seven. It was precisely because of the hardness and sharpness of this everyday realism that these people could feel safe in opening to inner worlds of perception, to the light within the light and the mountain behind the mountain. It is only when we are safely grounded on hard fact that we can safely open to regions beyond that of hard fact, which are as real as, indeed more real than, everyday reality. We are in our day proudly conscious of our realism and our openness of mind, but the truth is that we suffer in almost every domain from a crippling poverty of categories.

IV

Most of the hymns of praise of Christ in the *Carmina Gadelica* have a double movement: a movement reaching upwards towards the Father and source of creation *Ree na Nool*, and a movement downwards and inwards towards the womanhood and entirely human motherhood of Mary in her 'exceeding white purity of beauty'.

There is a very natural union of the vision of the cosmic Christ of transcendence, clothed in the glory of sun, moon and stars and surrounded by the angelic hierarchies of the great ancient theologian we call Dionysius the Areopagite, the 'Cosmic' Christ of Origen and Teilhard de Chardin on the one hand, and on the other, the simple domestic reality of the Child-bearing virgin and the vulnerable new-born baby who is forever the 'son of the loveliest Mary'. One of the great theological thinkers of our time, G. K. Chesterton, could never feel himself at home in his own heart with the transcendent Christ of high Anglicanism and had to find along the little roads of the world, specifically in a wild mountain landscape in Ireland, the God become man of his deepest needs and desires; the Christ of the transcendent Christologies came to him with the cold inhuman breath of an alien world. Who has not read treatises, heard sermons, on the transcendent saviour of judgement and righteousness and felt something of this chill and terror? Here Mary comes in all simplicity, all innocence, a girl-being in the truth and beauty of the eternal, unsullied feminine; and she brings to us the all-vulnerable generosity of that total sacrifice in which the mother becomes the only consort and companion of the man who is God (John 19.25). All this and much more than this shines forth in the Christ–Mary hymns of the *Carmina Gadelica*.

We are now in an atmosphere in which it is possible to speak in the right human way of the theme of love in this traditional hymn, a theme common in one way or another to almost all the hymns of the *Carmina Gadelica*. In the second part of the hymn, where transcendence becomes wedded to immanence with the appearance of the woman with her child, the God-encompassing true feminine, Christ is variously revealed as more lover than Lord, and finally as love itself in the divine-human heart and the flowing of the holy blood.

To begin with this last, the original Gaelic is *a chriosda chró-naoimhe*, which Carmichael englished as 'O Christ of the holy blood', though the original is strangely close to the *chroi-naomhtha* or *chroi-ro-naomtha* of Irish-Gaelic devotional literature. Dwelly's standard Gaelic–English dictionary (generally very respectful of Carmichael as a source) englishes *Cro-naomtha* as 'sacred heart'. Carmichael, who himself tended towards what is sometimes called Columban Christianity and cannot be claimed for either side of the Reformation divide, nevertheless knew well that, at a time when Scottish Presbyterianism routinely rejected Roman Catholicism as the most abominable superstition, he could have seemed a crypto-Catholic and would have avoided the phrase 'sacred heart' as *male sonans* to Protestant ears.[29] The main question that arises for the contemporary reader is the possible influence of the widespread eighteenth- and nineteenth-century devotion connected with St. Margaret Mary

[29] Nevertheless, where the context demands a more containing type of word, as in that unusual hymn entitled 'Soul-shrine' (I, no. 39, p. 93), Carmichael *does* use the language of the Sacred Heart devotion.

and Blessed Claude de la Columbière, SJ, and widely diffused by generations of Jesuit preachers and spiritual directors. This would help us to date the time of the composition of this noble and glowing Christmas hymn, but would still leave intact its roots in the very far past, as Carmichael and G. R. S. Maclean tend to claim. These deep roots may indeed have been watered at various times throughout the centuries, illustrating in a remarkable way Hans Georg Gadamer's thesis in *Truth and Method* that an ancient text must not be enclosed narrowly in its original *sitz-im-leben* but must be released into the ongoing stream of history.[30] This is indeed true of the whole Celtic tradition: its original truth as represented by the labours of historians and other scholars must be respected and never lost; but it must come alive in the present and it may be true that Carmichael's englishing of a certain phrase in a certain hymn might allow it to enter more easily into the stream of that Scottish Presbyterian hymnody in which everybody sings in the choir.

V

As the contemporary Christian makes or tries to make a living connection with this simple and profound hymn to Christ and 'Mary of graces', one phrase especially challenges understanding: it comes at the beginning of the third stanza, where Christ (at once transcendent and immanent) is invoked as 'Thou refuge of my love'. In what sense is Christ a refuge or protector of the love of the suppliant? What love is this? The suppliant's love of Christ? Of God? Of the neighbour? There is surely a clear call to try to connect here with the Gaelic original penned by Alexander Carmichael as he listened to Fiona MacDougal from Glen on the Isle of Barra recalling what she had heard as a young woman long ago in Morar. '*Chriosd, a comairc mo ruin*', she had intoned,

[30] H. Gadamer, *Truth and Method* (London: Sheed & Ward, 1988).

and Carmichael wrote it down as a faithful scribe and translated it as 'Christ, Thou refuge of my love'. *Comairc* is surely equivalent to 'refuge' or 'protector' and the theme of protection is central to nearly all these hymns as they link the three worlds of the human, the angelic–divine and the challenging ever-seductive world of the fallen spirits. Human love and human loving in their manifold vulnerability are especially in need of the ever-present protection of the transcendent world of Christ and the angels, and perhaps this is what is meant by invoking Christ as 'the refuge of my love'. Yet, *pace* Carmichael, who was a great scholar and a great Christian (though not, he would himself aver, *not* a mystic in any strong sense), it may be asked whether the word *ruin* here connotes 'mystery' or 'inwardness' rather than 'love' and relates to that spark or *scintilla* within of which the mystics such as Teresa speak. This spark is something very deep, very personal, secret and sacred; and it is the fruit, in the order of receptivity, of much active prayer and constant devotion. It is at this point that our hymn becomes heart-centred. It even becomes body-centred in the womb of Mary, in the holy blood of the heart of Christ. This is the region of that living spark or flame of love, the *llama de amor viva* of which John of the Cross speaks. In this Christmas hymn '*Sorchar nan Reul*', 'The Lightener of the Stars', we are listening to the deep music of one of the great hidden mystical streams of Christendom, of a Christendom always at prayer in so far as it is true to itself. This understanding does not at all depend on how we translate *ruin* or *comairc mo ruin*, for it sounds everywhere in the *Carmina Gadelica.* It shows its spark and its sparkle time and again, right through that hidden, long neglected world of Celtic spirituality.

9

NOSTALGIA FOR EDEN

George MacDonald's *Lilith*

I

George MacDonald (1824–1905) was known in his own day as a romantic and religious novelist, and also as a poet and preacher. As a minister of the kirk he did not commend himself to the traditional pattern – indeed, this was a main reason why he had to live by the pen – yet he remained all his life a deeply committed Christian in the Calvinist tradition of the greatness and majesty of God. Yet MacDonald's God did not stand for a closed, dogmatic, impenetrable heavens but for an open horizon, like dawn on the hills or across the sea, full of invitation and full of promise: the God of imagination, maker and archetypal image of human imagination.

In his long-ignored but now celebrated essay on 'The Imagination: Its Functions and Its Culture', written in 1867 but only published after the author's death (in *A Dish of Orts*, 1907), MacDonald freely admits the dangers of the faculty of imagination, especially in its early manifestations, yet claims that 'the imagination of man is made in the image of the imagination of God' and that 'a wise imagination which is the presence of the Spirit of God, is the best guide that man or woman can have'. These are strong statements and may at first sight seem rhetorical, but although the essay in which they occur is well garnished with rhetoric, yet his apotheosis of imagination is quite central to MacDonald's whole world as a writer and as a religious thinker.

It must be carefully noted that MacDonald speaks of 'the *wise* imagination'. This means that the imagination is not seen as somehow released from the control of thought and commitment, of all that has to be won by careful and balanced reflection, by connection with a living tradition personally appropriated. Imagination is indeed free, may indeed be defined as the free use of the images provided by observation and memory, but if it is to keep open to 'the presence of the Spirit of God', it must look ever upwards and outwards, away from narrow and narrowing selfishness and possessiveness; here especially it must be free. It can guide us safely on towards the land of heart's desire, but only if our desiring opens out and releases itself from the bondage of egoism and self-indulgence, from lifeless dogmatism and merely comfortable commitment. Only for the 'pure of heart' of the gospels, only for those who have achieved something of that 'greatness of soul' of which Aristotle spoke, is this voyage made in accordance with the fresh and fragrant winds of the Spirit of God. Only thus can we launch forth on the wide waters of imagination to seek the lost paradise of Genesis, the Land of the Young (*Teernanogue*) of Celtic folklore.

Only today, after centuries of scientific materialism, are we beginning to rediscover this world. Kathleen Raine, Edwin Muir, Yeats and AE are heralds of this world. So was George MacDonald in his understanding of the reality of the inner world discovered by 'the wise imagination' as the presence of the Spirit of God.

II

Let us now look at the book in which MacDonald most strikingly expressed the reality and substantiality of this world: *Lilith*, the fantasy novel written near the end of his life, the mature expression of his reality-world of imagination.

In *Lilith* MacDonald recovers, in his own way and in the images and traditions available to him, the original world of Eden, the Paradise of innocent and holy love, the Land of the Young. So it is that the children, the Little Ones, play a central role in the story; so, too, man and woman are naked and unashamed as Adam and Eve before the Fall; so too man and nature live harmoniously together. Yet, for all this vision of innocence and freshness, evil has come: Lilith is evil, and so are the people of the city over which she rules (C. S. Lewis uses the same scenario in *The Lion, the Witch and the Wardrobe*). And so the novel becomes a story of redemption in which Adam and Christ are one. The story insistently demands a feminine saviour as well, but MacDonald's strong residual Calvinism does not easily accommodate a Virgin Mother as the New Eve; however, this Eve-Mary figure is not far away at the end.

One can scarcely use the word 'erotic' of the novel, as this word has too many ambiguous overtones. It is, perhaps, more sensitive and more accurate to speak of the holy force of *Eros-Agapé* that vibrates through all creation and must have its source in the original dyad that becomes a triad or trinity in which *Eros-Agapé* is the binding force and the pure fiery expression of eternal love. *Lilith* is at one level the working out of the mending and saving of this basic harmony of *Eros-Agapé* that has been broken and dishonoured by a primal fault, a sundering of primal love. In his exuberance and openness MacDonald exemplifies the type of human being who has a deep nostalgia for Eden, the kind of nostalgia that can be marvellously creative and constructive or, misused or misunderstood, can lead to tragic aberrations and misunderstandings.

But surely *Lilith* is first and last a work of fantasy? It may have this or that lesson on applicability; it may show forth certain characteristics of MacDonald, and even find an echo in many people who share the author's nostalgia for Eden. Yet, for all that, must it not be admitted that MacDonald 'made it all up' as he went along? It is fiction and has, like all the best fiction, much to challenge and stimulate us, much to help us to interpret life's moods and vicissitudes. When all is said, MacDonald himself must have been conscious that it all proceeded from his own imagination, perhaps indeed a 'wise imagination', but imagination after all.

Before we accept this seemingly sensible interpretation of what MacDonald was about and what *Lilith* is about, it is well to recall what has been said about 'the imaginal world' and the sense in which those 'ancient springs' of which Kathleen Raine speaks may be flowing through what is deepest in MacDonald's fantasy 'fiction'. In the essay already cited, MacDonald has a remarkable paragraph on the creativity of imagination. He asks whether the imaginative writer – clearly he means the writer of 'wise' imagination – really *creates* what he imagines, the 'thought-forms' in which he embodies his vision. And he replies:

> Such embodiments are not the result of the man's intention, or of the operation of his conscious nature. His feeling is that they are given to him; that from the vast unknown, where time and space are not, they suddenly appear in luminous writing upon the wall of his consciousness. Can it be correct, then, to say that he created them? Nothing less so, as it seems to us. But can we not say that they are the creation of the unconscious portion of his nature? Yes, provided we can understand that that which is the individual, the man, can know, and not know that it knows, can create and yet be ignorant that virtue has gone out of it. From that unknown region we grant they come, but not by its own blind working. Nor, even were it so, could any amount of such production, where no will was concerned, be dignified with the name of creation. But God sits in that chamber of our being in which the candle of our consciousness goes out in darkness, and sends forth from thence wonderful gifts into the light of that understanding which is His candle. Our hope lies in no

> most perfect mechanism even of the spirit, but in the wisdom wherein we live and move and have our being. Thence we hope for endless forms of beauty informed of truth. If the dark portion of our own being were the origin of our imaginations, we might well fear the apparition of such monsters as would be generated in the sickness of a decay which could never feel – only declare – a slow return towards primeval chaos. But the Maker is our Light.

There is no doubt but that MacDonald's Calvinism 'shows' in this paragraph. As a Calvinist he does not wish to give any credit or merit to fallen (or even redeemed) man. The absolute Divine initiative must be protected at all costs, especially here where there is question of that part of man which most of all might go its own way. More especially, man must be protected against the dark side of his imagination. G. K. Chesterton, an admirer and indeed to a real extent a disciple of MacDonald, found refuge from the dark side of his imagination not in Calvinism but in the infallible Roman Catholic Church. Indeed it could be argued that the extreme Calvinism of the Scots and the extreme Catholicism of the Irish are equally ways of coping with the dark side of the Celtic imagination.

But once imagination is (for MacDonald) linked to its source in God, it becomes a source of revelation, a way of listening and learning. No more than Kathleen Raine does MacDonald claim that his inner world of imagination is free of all subjective elements. Not only in the general sense but also in a personal sense, his vision of Eden is deeply conditioned by his own experience and his theology. But this has to do with the limits of visions rather than with the inner world that really and truly calls us to enter it, to find our way in it, and indeed to find God 'walking' in it. Neither MacDonald nor Kathleen Raine will claim that this vision of the inner world, the *mundus imaginalis*, is other than intermittent, seen in flashes and glimpses, yet something more than Eliot's 'hints and guesses', and in some people somehow always present as 'the mountain behind the mountain'. Perhaps we might recall the words of Francis Thompson, a genuine poet-visionary in the great tradition, whose genius has been occluded by some modernist and post-modernist literary critics:

> Yet ever and anon a trumpet sounds
> From the hid battlements of Eternity;
> Those shaken mists a space unsettle, then
> Round the half-glimpsèd turrets slowly wash again.[31]

George MacDonald's Land of Youth, the lost Paradise of innocent and holy love, where all is well, is never more than half-glimpsed, but this glimpse perhaps opens on to that real world of which our everyday world is but a faint image. The man of 'wise imagination' sees this image in its eternal source.

[31] 'The Hound of Heaven', *The Poems of Francis Thompson* (London: Oxford University Press, 1938), p. 93.

10

THE MYSTERY OF LAMENTATION

I

The mystery of lamentation is like all the great mysteries, such as death and the holy force of human sexuality, essentially beyond the control and imperialism of human understanding. It has about it the three signs that mark all mysteries. It is awe-inspiring; it opens out to infinity; it walks in its own light and so it resists being fully seen in any light from any other star. We must approach its shrine with deepest reverence, since we are walking on holy ground. Within this sanctuary we speak in whispers as nuns do before the altar of the holy sacrament of the Body of Christ. We are here to pray, to open our inner eyes to a light other than the light of common day, other than the light of understanding, nearer perhaps to the light of poetry and the light that illuminates the world of the visual artist.

We shall approach this mystery in three zones or spheres of its manifestation: the Christian Scriptures, the holy places of the Celtic Christian tradition and finally in the light of the great English poets of the Isles of the North. There is question only of *approaching*; should we try to come too near we shall lose the delicate lights of the mystery of lamentation which above all else we must not lose or relinquish.

II

The Christian Scriptures include the New Testament, witnessing to the Christ event, and the Old Testament, witnessing to the preparation and background of the Christ event. Central to the Old Testament, though not quite *the* centre of it – this is rather the book of Isaiah – is the book of Jeremiah and the book of Lamentations. The Latin translation of this book is surely one of the greatest achievements of St. Jerome: the words seem to be *asking* for the singing mode of the human voice. This has been provided by the medieval masters of Christian liturgical music as it is completed by the musical renderings of Second Isaiah.

It has been said by a modern philosopher, Theodor Adorno, that poetry is impossible after Auschwitz, though he admits that silence will not do either. What is perhaps possible is the poetry of lamentation and the poetry of the afflicted servant of Deutero-Isaiah. One thing seems certain: there cannot be a poetry of Easter and Resurrection that reaches to the depths of human experience without a poetry and a music of Good Friday and the Holocaust. At the depths of human experience in its Christian mode there must be the prayer that faces the crucifying *peirasmos* and the utterly terrifying *ponēros* of the great Christian prayer, the Lord's Prayer.

The prayer of Jesus in its heights and depths: that is the great central mystery of the New Testament. It is a depth experience that goes down into deeps beyond human imagining and ascends into heights equally beyond human imagining. The depths of anguish and agony are revealed to us for a moment in the accounts of the agony in the garden of Gethsemane, the place of total lamentation. It is also revealed to us on the Mount of the Transfiguration, where 'his face did shine as the sun and his garments became white as snow'. This dark lamentation and this dazzling glory form a kind of vocal scale that sounds all through the New Testament and reaches back to the expectational world of the Old Testament.

Let us listen for a moment to a voice that sounds again and again in the Old Testament: it rises up clear and unmistakeable in Jer. 31.15 (RSV):

A voice is heard in Ramah,
Lamentation and bitter weeping.
Rachel is weeping for her children;
She refuses to be comforted for her children,
Because they are not.

Clear and piercing this cry is repeated, at once echo and repetition, at the beginning of the New Testament, at Matt. 2.17–18 and it waits all the time in the background until it rises up from Jesus-Emmanuel at the moment of his death, the great cry (*boē megalē*) set down by all four evangelists and by St. Paul. Out of the depths of this superhuman lamentation, possible only against this background, comes forth the breathless breathing of 'He is risen': he is not here in the tomb, he is risen, and walking in power and glory into the promised Kingdom.

What is remarkable and surely central to the whole Christ-event is that the shining glory of the Transfiguration has its source and centre in the Crucifixion. 'And behold, two men talked with him, Moses and Elijah who appeared in glory and spoke of his departure, which he was to accomplish at Jerusalem' (Luke 9.30–31). The voice in Ramah, the voice of lamentation, is finally fulfilled in the voice of glory. Dimly in dark contemplation we are aware that lamentation and glory belong together. In all lamentation, the eternal radiance of glory begins to appear, a radiance that cannot otherwise appear. This is the inner movement of joy hidden within the voice of lamentation. It is at the very well-springs of the Paschal mystery and what has been called the *Triduum Sanctum* which is the crowning glory of the Christian liturgical mystery.

The liturgy of the *Triduum Sanctum*, of Holy Week and Easter, is all in the mode of commemoration, all aimed at the fulfilment of the eucharistic words of Christ-Saviour: Do this in memory of me. Implicitly the divinity of human memory is affirmed as on a par with the two other eternal dimensions of manwomanhood, intelligence and will. They are all equally mirroring in manwomanhood the holy and undivided Trinity. But just as the Father, in relation to the Son and Holy Spirit, stands for source and origination, so too in the inner human trinity, memory, imaging the divine source, has a certain priority not of glory or dignity but of origination. All this was somehow revealed to the great Augustine, as we can read in the tenth book of the *Confessions.* And all this is in the background both of Augustine's golden commentaries on the Psalms and of the monastic assimilation of the Psalms into the everyday of Christian contemplation and action.

III

At the everyday level we may be in a small way affected by the penumbrae or shadowings that attend on the various senses of seeing and hearing and the rest, but a kind of necessity of common sense urges us strongly to close down firmly the shutters that are tightly excluding these imaginal worlds of second sight, second hearing and the rest. That part of the mighty world of eye and ear that our imaginal faculties 'half-create' – the word is that of William Wordsworth – is firmly kept at bay as we go about our ordinary world of 'getting and spending'. We miss 'the many splendoured thing' that is almost desperately trying to reveal itself at the limits and vestibules of our everyday perceiving selves. Yet is there not something just beneath the surface in each of us that rises up to meet the words of St. Paul when he speaks of all nature groaning in travail as it awaits a further revelation at the limits of perception (Rom. 8.22, 23)?

Now it is to this liminal, imaginal threshold world of hearing that lamentation belongs. There are sounds here and a sounding of the depths that no photograph, no scientific sonic apparatus can pick up. It is the world of the waves and the winds and the wild sea-mew, the birds from another world as it seems, that circle our coasts from St. Kilda to Skellig Michael. It is within this lamentation of all nature wailing together that we must try to understand the Celtic echoing and amplification of the Hebrew songs of Lamentations.

Scholars tell us that the songs of that extraordinary literary composition called the book of Lamentations had a special place in the Jewish liturgy and that certain women traditionally sang them. 'These dirges were of a ritual character and were normally uttered by a professionally trained class of women' (see Peake's *Commentary, in loco*). The voices of these women are still with us in the Celtic Keening tradition.

I shall look at some examples of Gaelic Keening in the Celtic tradition, one from Ireland and one from Scotland and one, finally, from an Irish writer of fiction, Liam O'Flaherty of the western Aran Islands.

One of the most interesting and attractive features about the celebrated anthologist of the *Golden Treasury of Songs and Lyrics*, Francis Palgrave, is that his book contains very many fine dirges or lamentations, mostly composed by unknown or little known women, though Sir Walter Scott does come in boldly now and then with Pibrochs and Coronachs. It must be said that Palgrave has ensured a certain modest immortality for these women: Jane Elliot, Margaret Oliphant (Lady Nairn) and Jane Lindsay (who wrote that most heart-rending personal elegy 'Auld Robin Gray'), a short list but enough to sound in 'Braid Scots' a voice as pure as the voices of the women who sang the ancient Hebrew Lamentations. Let us look at one of them: Jane Elliot's 'Lament for Flodden'. It needs a woman's singing voice, such as that of Ellen Wycherley or Karen Matheson or the legendary Kitty McLeod, to do it any kind of vocal justice, but here are a few stanzas of it.

I've heard them lilting at our ewe-milking,
    Lasses a' lilting before dawn o' day;
But now they are moaning on ilka green loaning –
    The Flowers of the Forest are a' wede away.

At e'en, in the gloaming, nae younkers are roaming
'Bout stacks wi' the lasses at bogle to play;
But ilk ane sits drearie, lamenting her dearie –
The Flowers of the Forest are weded away.

We'll hear nae mair lilting at the ewe-milking;
Women and bairns are heartless and wae;
Sighing and moaning on ilka green loaning –
The Flowers of the Forest are a' wede away.

The seventeenth-century lament for Art O'Leary, 'Keena Airt ui laoire' by Eileen O'Connell, Art's wife, expresses a personal grief with enormous passion and poignancy. After two hundred years it is still alive with the warmth of grief and the beating of a human heart that is still fluttering against the bars of mortality. You can still hear the sobbing of this woman's voice affirming by its very intensity the triumph of memory over forgetfulness, of life over death. It is all a phenomenon of light and of the source from which the light is coming. This light which haloes the hero and banishes his enemies into the outer darkness shines out of a source that rises beyond past, present and future. All true beauty escapes time: this the genius of John Keats understood and tried to find words and images to endow with concrete form. 'A thing of beauty is a joy for ever', he said, and the thing of beauty that is the 'Lament for Art O'Leary' rises above the corrosion of time; words come and go like human breath, but within the word is its kernel of light and this kernel is beyond the mortal condition.

Eileen Dubh rages at those sly and conspiring enemies who treacherously slay her beautiful man, but the lament is not at all swallowed up by the anger; this simply takes its place within a kind of diapason of emotion. Indeed a lament tends to lose and let go of its divine dimension and its mysterious releasing power if it turns to anger: in that direction it can only burn itself out. It must endeavour to preserve that purity of grief and humble tears that form a pathway towards the human heart of God Incarnate.

There is in the course of Irish and Anglo-Irish literature an underground river which has been called the literature of the dispossessed. It goes underground with James Clarence Mangan, bypasses Joyce and Yeats, and surfaces again variously with Daniel Corkery, Padraig Colum and Liam O'Flaherty. O'Flaherty's *Famine* was written in the 1930s and reprinted many times.[32] It was hailed by Anthony Burgess as 'telling the kind of truth only a major writer of fiction is capable of portraying'.

Among much else O'Flaherty tries to portray the traditional Irish wake (James Joyce later found the key to his dreamworld in it, writing a quite unreadable book, *Finnegans Wake*). It is a wake of the famine days and the Keening expresses some of the terror and desolation of a calamity that took a whole community beyond the limits of endurance. Yet, and this is painfully impressive, the ancient decencies must be observed even if it means leaving the household penniless and in starvation.

Far different, yet very impressive and even terrifying to a boy of twelve, was the Keening at the wake of my grandfather sixty years ago. The old man's daughter-in-law, Bridget Kelly, knelt by the dead man and wailed and wailed until my boy's heart nearly stopped. But nobody shushed me away, for this was the way of life and death and it was better that I should face it. Nowadays, when children are protected from getting either a kiss or a clout from life, this would not do at all and all the normal dangerous human emotions are put in a deep freeze with the lemonades and coca cola.

But I am beginning to moralise, so I had better stop, firmly leaving to one side one of the deepest problems of our time, the death of the *Ban Keenta*, the 'mourning woman' whom there was no-one left to mourn.

[32] See paperback edition (Dublin: Wolfhound Press, 1994).

IV

I have tried to show that lamentation keening has been given a place of importance, even central importance, in the Judaeo-Christian Scriptures and also in the Celtic understanding and absorption of these writings over the centuries. The great enduring sorrows and calamities of the Jewish and Celtic peoples have given depth and cosmic power to the lamentation literature of these people.

Our focusing on these people and their literature is, however, concerned ultimately not with these or any special people but with the universal *humanum* manwomanhood in one of its most precious dimensions, and this kind of study is of little use or relevance unless it has what may be termed a heuristic purpose, that is, unless it opens our minds and hearts to the place and prevalence of lamentation in the universal human story. One could do this by looking at the great classical writers, epic poets and tragedians who stand forever at the gateway of European literature and who are, every single one of them, great rivers of tears. But it seems more friendly and more just to open up our topic to one of the great wonders of the eternal *humanum* which is English literature and more generally literature in the English language.

I have already focused on Palgrave's *Golden Treasury of Songs and Lyrics*, a collection republished, and updated again and again since it first appeared in 1861. There the theme of lamentation is given a place of honour and is, whether by accident or design, quite disproportionately represented by women writers. Somehow the voices of the great men of English poetry, of Shakespeare, Milton and the rest, do not have quite the same quality of immediate, intimately piercing, personal experience that attends the voices of the women. They show forth *meditation* on human sorrow and calamity rather than the direct immediate voice of human sorrow, naked and unashamed. A kind of philosophical dignity and distance clothes the naked human spirit stricken by grief, taken out of itself by sorrow. From Shakespeare to Milton, to Tennyson, to Eliot, the literature written in English expressive of grief and 'the tears of things' is elegaic rather than lamentational and shines with philosophical rather than emotional light and glory.

Let us look at what is perhaps its most perfect or at least its most typical expression, Thomas Gray's 'Elegy written in a Country Churchyard'.

It is doubtful whether this marvellous magical, almost uniquely felicitous effusion was in fact *written* in a country churchyard at the coming on of night, but it was no doubt conceived there and even planned in its main structure. And whatever spirit it was that took hold of this Cambridge don, it had not its dwelling in Cambridge or any other academic milieu. Somehow, from somewhere, the muse appeared, the blessed spirit of inspiration, and Thomas Gray, as even his formidable critic Samuel Johnson admitted, wrote something beyond all criticism. Even the criticism of lack of immediacy falls down as one is bewitched by those heavenly couplets:

> For who, to dumb forgetfulness a prey,
> This pleasing anxious being e'er resign'd
> Left the warm precincts of the cheerful day,
> Nor cast one longing lingering look behind?

Here beyond all academic sophistication *pathos* asserts itself and pathos is that divine something which no angel, no lesser god can feel. Only the divine heart that is also human, totally human, can feel it. It is the authentic inimitable Christian thing that can only flow forth in its full mountain purity from the hill of Calvary . . .

11

THE WORLD OF THE INNER SELF

I

In the discovery of the Face of the Father in both Augustine and Patrick there is a deep tenderness and a piercing of the heart or affectivity in which all the outer senses as well as the inner senses of memory and imagination become, as it were, deeply tinged and coloured, and even raised to a new dimension, by fire and light somehow received from the Source itself by a kind of outflowing and inflowing. For this the affectivity has been prepared by asceticism and detachment. This asceticism of the senses, detached from the pull or gravitation of sensuality and that self-indulgence that dies into its own fulfilment away from the Source, finds a new fulfilment beyond the desert of detachment and a new flowering of memory and imagination and of the five external senses. This is the way of the spiritual or spiritualised senses spoken of by Origen and taken up later by Bonaventure and the Franciscan tradition (by St. Thomas, too) and in modern times by Poulain and the early Karl Rahner, in his pre-Heidegger days. It is this spirituality of the senses as it arises spontaneously within him that gives Patrick's *Confession* its warmth and tenderness as he speaks of his relationship with the Father, the Son and the Holy Spirit. I shall return to Patrick's *Confession* in a moment and to certain passages in it. First, however, I want to look at two key passages in Augustine's *Confessions* (10.6(8) and 10.27(34)) in which the mystical doctrine of the spiritual senses is clearly expressed, though it must be said that this understanding of human perceiving animates the whole of the *Confessions* from first to last.

II

Let us look at the first part of Chapter 6, Book 10 in the Penguin translation of a certain Fr. Pine-Coffin, who is fortunately much livelier than his name seems to promise; this rather obvious sally may serve to remind us what a very lively piece of writing the *Confessions* is. Patrick's *Confession* is lively too, but while Augustine's *Confessions* has the liveliness of unexampled eloquence, Patrick's has the liveliness of an almost incoherent earnestness.

> My love of you, O Lord, is not some vague feeling: it is positive and certain. Your word struck into my heart and from that moment I loved you. Besides this, all about me, heaven and earth and all that they contain proclaim that I should love you, and their message never ceases to sound in the ears of all mankind, so that there is no excuse for any not to love you. But, more than all this, *you will show pity on those whom you pity; you will show mercy where you are merciful*; for if it were not for your mercy, heaven and earth would cry your praises to deaf ears.
>
> But what do I love when I love my God? Not material beauty or beauty of a temporal order; not the brilliance of earthly light, so welcome to our eyes; not the sweet melody of harmony and song; not the fragrance of flowers, perfumes, and spices; not manna or honey; not limbs such as the body delights to embrace. It is not these that I love when I love my God. And yet, when I love him, it is true that I love a light of a certain kind, a voice, a perfume, a food, an embrace; but they are of the kind that I love in my inner self, when my soul is bathed in light that is not bound by space; when it listens to sound that never dies

> away; when it breathes fragrance that is not borne away on the wind; when it tastes food that is never consumed by the eating; when it clings to an embrace from which it is not severed by fulfilment of desire. This is what I love when I love my God.[33]

There is here a very clear rejection of the way of the five exterior senses, followed immediately by an equally clear acceptance of each and all of them as they are reflected or re-lived within the inner self, a self (it seems clear) purified of the materiality and corruptibility of corruptible matter, that *materia prima corporalis* or *terrestris* that is always shedding its shapeliness in the restlessness of that privative principle that haunts it.

In this passage Augustine goes through all the five senses: seeing, hearing, smelling (fragrance), tasting (manna or honey) and finally touching: *tactus.* Sexuality for the moralists of the Great Tradition (Aquinas, for example) was deeply connected with the 'joys of touch', *delectationes tactus.* And of course Augustine was acutely conscious of the attraction of these 'joys of touch' and of the need to take a very firm negative line with this form of sensual experience. Yet in this regard it is necessary to ponder deeply on a text like the present, by no means unique in Augustine's writing, in which that bodily touch so deeply involved with sexual eros is spoken of positively and appreciatively as on a level with music to the ears and honey to the taste. Obviously, something within all of these sensual joys is not only 'redeemable' by way of asceticism and the great cardinal virtue of temperance but blossoms afresh in the pure soil of the inner self.

We are here in the world of the anointing of the Holy Spirit, which must be carefully and even prayerfully understood. At its centre it is a mystical or receptive experience connected with

[33] *Saint Augustine: Confessions,* trans. S. R. Pine-Coffin (Harmondsworth: Penguin, 1974), pp. 211–12.

prayer. It brings a deep glow to the mind and heart, and it flows into the bodily being, especially the sense of touch. You find it in the *hagion philēma* or 'holy kiss' of the first Christians (see 1 Cor. 16.20). As a touch it is clear that it was present in the brotherhood of Socrates when the sage himself slept with Alcibiades in complete chastity in the *Symposium*. Of course it can easily become abused or misunderstood, as has happened in our day, it would seem, to those hapless men who are drawn by the innocent affectionateness of boys and girls into destructive relationships. It demands an asceticism totally focused on the Source.

III

We now come to what is perhaps the most famous passage in the whole vast array of the works of Augustine of Hippo which he left behind in bundles tied with strings when he died at Hippo Regius on August 28th, 430. This is the passage that begins 'Late have I loved Thee O Beauty ever ancient and ever new', and it goes on to tell us how he had looked for the 'Beauty ever ancient and ever new' outside himself in the beautiful things of the world of men and women and the goods of the earth, and so failed miserably, for God as the Source of all Beauty was within his own human soul.

But if we stop at this point all we have is an elegant general statement of the truth that the Kingdom of Heaven is within, as if our author had taken it up and set it down like a chair. If, however, we look back from Chapter 27 to Chapter 6 of the same tenth book and the passage just analysed, and then apply this to what the rest of Chapter 27 has to say, briefly but with the brevity of a nutshell, we shall find a whole new world opening up before us. For what we find is that the soul opens to the face of God not simply as spirit-soul but as sense-soul in all its fivefold sensibility. It is not (as in Chapter 6) that the sensibility moves upward into the spirit-realm but that (the Holy Spirit of) God moves downward to find a new response within each of the senses. We are in the realm of those inner locutions heard by the inner spiritual ear, an inner odour as of an inner fragrance, a new marvellous sense of a spiritual presence, a new taste that suffers no satiety.

In all this as it appears or reappears in Chapter 27 and speaks or sings of the beauty ever ancient and ever new, the human self is almost totally receptive in a receptivity more passive than active, whereas in Chapter 6 the receptive soul was seen as more active than passive, albeit no less receptive. In this sense both passages belong to the world of mystical prayer, what later Teresa and the Carmelite tradition was to call 'supernatural' prayer.

IV

We are here in the world of mystical imagination, where the free power of imagination, unbound by space and time and fed by the springs of human affectivity, connects with that Platonic 'light above the mind' which in Chapter 10 of Book 7 centres and focuses the whole ascending vision of the *Confessions.* The great Platonic vision of the Transcendental Ideas, the five lamps of the mind, opens upwards to 'the metaphysics of Exodus' and downward to the Incarnate Logos and the child in the manger.

This fusion of horizons set down in Chapter 10 of Book 7 of the *Confessions* looks back to the mighty vision of the first chapter of the Gospel of John, but it finds its proper location in the human heart and its affective springs in the mysterious world of the inner self, here sketched briefly and elegantly by Augustine, the greatest of rhetoricians. Those who have ears to hear can only listen in amazement to his song.

Far different is the song that Patrick sings in the northern lands of darkness (Scotland) and winter (Hibernia, Ireland).

V

Let us recall paragraph 16 of Patrick's *Confession.*

> But after I had come to Ireland I daily used to feed cattle, and I prayed frequently during the day; the love of God and the fear of Him increased more and more, and faith became stronger, and the spirit was stirred; so that in one day I said about a hundred prayers, and in the night nearly the same; so that I used even to remain in the woods and in the mountain; before daylight I used to rise to prayer, through snow, through frost, through rain, and felt no harm; nor was there any slothfulness in me, as I now perceive, because the spirit was then fervent within me.

Now while a certain rhetorical enhancing of the narrative was second nature to Augustine, it had no place at all in Patrick's bare narrative. When he numbers his prayers we feel that he is not so much using round numbers as approximate numbers, give or take one or two. This strange young man, keeper of cows and pigs in cold winter days and nights, has been somehow transformed into the keeper of flocks of prayers winging their way between earth and heaven, as the dawn breaks in beauty ever ancient and ever new across an Irish hillside. There is a great fire burning within this boy growing into manhood, so that he does not feel the touch of snow or ice nor the slanting sudden showers. We are in the presence of prayer, not the painful plod of active or ascetical prayer but the glow and conflagration of that receptive prayer in which the suppliant is taken up, taken over by a higher power.

There is about all this the passion and rhythms of first love, of the human spirit in the full flush of youthful enthusiasm. We must pass on to a paragraph towards the end of the *Confession* to encounter this love in its maturity, beyond all excitement, deeply rooted within the firm fertile depths of the good ground of the parable of the seed, that ground which is the only soil of sacrifice from Abraham to St. Paul.

And so paragraph 59 runs:

> And if I have ever imitated anything good on account of my God, whom I love, I pray Him to grant me, that with those proselytes and captives, I may pour out my blood for His name's sake, even although I myself may even be deprived of burial, and my corpse most miserably be torn limb from limb by dogs, or by wild beasts, or that the fowls of heaven should devour it. I believe most certainly that if this should happen to me, I shall have gained both soul and body. Because without any doubt we shall rise in that day in the brightness of the sun, that is, in the glory of Jesus Christ, our Redeemer, as 'sons of the living God' (Hosea 1.10) and 'joint-heirs with Christ' (Rom. 8.17) and to be 'conformable to His image' (Rom. 8.29) for 'of Him, and through Him, and in Him' (Rom. 11.36) we shall reign.

Here the corruptible body passes through a kind of immolation, which might equally have come by earth-burial or cremation, into a new sphere or region of reality in which the composite body–soul self shines forth in the brightness of the sun and the glory of the bodily resurrection of Jesus Christ. This for Patrick would be the last day, which he saw as coming soon now that, through his Irish mission, the Christian gospel was preached to all nations and to the ends of the earth.

And here Patrick goes on to say strange things about the physical sun in our daily skies. This sun is corruptible and will fail in accordance with the Christian apocalyptic vision, but the true sun, *solem verum Christum*, will never perish but will, in the words of 1 John 2.17, 'continue forever'. Here we are in the full reality of the world of the physical incorruptible or that 'imaginal' world which was to become part of the tradition of Irish and Celtic Christianity. Here the hidden virtuality of physical perception opens up to the world of the Resurrection. This world does not reveal itself by way of ordinary observation but rather by intimation and 'arguments that cannot be proven', a way of knowing not far from Newman's Illative Sense, which rings its own bell of certainty for those attuned to it, those whose life has become a waiting in prayer.

Patrick's *Confession*, as well as Augustine's *Confessions*, is the statement of a Christian faith that mediates a great mystery and this can never be more than a human mediation of something essentially beyond human ken in our present state. Necessarily and rightly, Augustine and Patrick can only 'prophesy in part' (*ek merous*, 1 Cor. 13.9) and the mystery remains. But these *Confessions* are also ways of prayer, ways in which a great spirit has sought the face of the Source of life and love and truth, and shows us the way to truth by way of continuing humble prayer wherein alone answers are to be found.

12

BEYOND THE CONCEPT OF HERESY: THE CASE OF PELAGIUS

I

The greatest work of Pelagius (*c.* 360–430 AD), at least of those that have come down to us, is his *Commentary on St. Paul's Epistles*, and we may take two statements from this Commentary as providing a clear mirror of the commentator's temper of mind and approach to Christian revelation. One is his comment on 1 Cor. 14.1, where the text reads, as it sums up all that has been said in Chapter 13 in praise of charity, *sequamini caritatem.* This is translated 'make love your aim' by the RSV and says literally in the Greek original 'follow after charity'. Pelagius comments: *omni conatu ipsam sequimini quia in vestra est potestate*, literally: 'follow charity with all your strength, for this is in your power to do'. Pelagius is not saying that it is possible to do this or anything else without God's help, but that this help is available to man by his creation as the creature of a good God who saw from the beginning that his creation was good, 'very good' in fact (Gen. 1.31). In this matter of original goodness Pelagius was more profoundly critical of Manichaeism than ever Augustine was; indeed, the ageing Augustine was quite vulnerable to accusations that he had never quite shed the Manichaeism of his youth.

The other text is from Rom. 8.10, where the Latin text reads: *si autem Christus in vobis est, corpus quidem mortuum est propter peccatum, spiritus vero vivit propter iustitiam*, which the RSV translates: 'But if Christ is in you, although your bodies are dead because of sin, your spirits are alive because of righteousness.' The comment of Pelagius begins *si Christum imitamini*, thus putting the emphasis not on the *presence* of Christ within man (i.e. by grace) but rather on our own activity in the *imitation* of Christ. We are looking at the great divide between the Catholic theology of the imitation of Christ and the Reform theology of substitution according to which Christ is already, once and for all, *our* justification, once we believe in him, and all 'good works' such as pilgrimages and monasticism are condemned, as also is any re-enactment by mere human beings of the once and for all sacrifice of Christ: no Mass, therefore, though the Last Supper may be commemorated as a shared *agapé* meal. The great sixteenth-century reformer, Martin Luther, who was an Augustinian friar, went in this direction; opposed to Luther was Ignatius of Loyola who led a whole army of men (and women too) along the path of the imitation of Christ by way of the Spiritual Exercises. It was a follower of Ignatius named Molina who tried to reconcile Pelagius' activism with Augustinian passivity by way of a new doctrine of the divine omniscience and divine predestination.

II

At the centre of the controversy between Augustine and Pelagius (especially in his follower, Julian of Eclanum, an Italian bishop) was (and is) the question of original sin or the great shadow that lies across human life and human history, the recognition or supposition of which is by no means confined to Christianity. In one form or another, explicitly or implicitly if only by reaction, it has affected the lives of all of us, and I shall proceed by speaking of it in terms of my own experience as a boy in an ancient Catholic tradition born and brought up in the south-west of Ireland over seventy years ago. I lived on a mountain side looking down on the church or chapel in the valley, and I have already set it down that the chapel and the mountain spoke to me with diverse though not contradictory voices, voices each belonging to its own world, and perhaps too far apart to contradict each other. In a way I think Pelagius Britto, whether Irish or Welsh or English or Scots, had also something of the experience of these two voices, and that all went well with him until, far away in the torrid climate of Italy and North Africa, he tried to reconcile them.

Now one of the things the chapel said to me was that there is such a thing as original sin, and it provided me with a definition of that which has lain peacefully all these years in the storehouse of memory. For I was a bright wee lad and could sing it out in one breath when the teacher or priest asked 'What is original sin?' 'Itisthesinweinheritfromourfirstparentsandbywhichweare conceivedandbornchildrenofwrath.' This, I say, rested peacefully in my memory all through the vicissitudes of adolescence and young manhood, all through my seven years of training for the priesthood, complete with several degrees, all through my years of priesthood, right up to this day. I understood it in a notional way, assented to it, studied its background in Scripture and tradition, even at times wrote about it and saw how the catechism answer connected with the catechism of the Council of Trent and mainline Catholic orthodoxy.

Nevertheless, when today I look at it squarely and let its significance sink in, I realise almost with a shock that I never really believed it. It never became part of me as mind-set and life-attitude as in truth it is, or was, meant to be by those who set it down as part of the Irish Maynooth catechism based on the catechism of the Council of Trent. Rather did I absorb from my mountain a temper of mind, a feeling for life that can only be called Pelagian. Certainly the chapel was redolent of the most firm Catholic, i.e. *Roman* Catholic, orthodoxy, so much so that one could almost smell it and feel it all around as a gentle, comforting, yet all-demanding presence that might even take over the whole of life, as in truth it may be said to have done when, pondering long thoughts through a long night, I decided to become a priest. Yet all this time, and even now, my temper of mind, my attitude to myself, to others and to the great source of us all has remained Pelagian, inasmuch as it never *really* assented to what the catechism was saying in telling me I was conceived and born a child of wrath.

For what, after all, *is* a child of wrath? Whose wrath? Why? Who did what to cause, call forth this wrath? Of course, bright boy that I was, I knew the answer pat. Adam and Eve incurred the wrath of God because together they disobeyed him. Eve was tricked by Satan in the shape of a serpent, and she pulled Adam along with her, and all their children right to this day share in this disobedience. That is why they all need to be washed clean in baptism and the sooner the better, for if they should die without being cleansed they go to limbo and are forever shut out from the light of Heaven, because they are still children of wrath.

All this I accepted; it was part of what the chapel said to me. But it never became real for me. The mountain did not contradict it; the mountain made no statement about it. Yet the mountain, its rocks and its streams, its valleys of wild myrtle, its uplands of heather and gorse – all this and more was massively *there*, and within it I was there in my human responsibility of good and evil, troubled not by Adam's sin but by my own, certain that I was free, certain that I could use my freedom to rise up to Heaven or descend into Hell. As I became familiar with literature, with the classics and with the English poets and writers, with the Gaelic and Anglo-Irish authors, I saw ever more clearly that something called me to goodness and glory and that I was free to say 'yes' or 'no', though I did need help from above and I had to ask for this in all humility. As I entered into my maturity I came to admire Augustine, as I think everybody who really reads him must admire him, but in my experience and temper of mind

I was with Pelagius and his rugged insistence on nature and freedom.

I also began to see that Augustine's doctrine of the Fall and original sin was very much his own, largely coloured by his own experience of moral breakdown and connected with a deep residual dualism of soul and body left over from his nine years as a Manichee. His *massa damnata* theology came neither from the New Testament nor from tradition, and might indeed be connected with Neoplatonic emanationism applied illegitimately to the moral sphere, i.e. seeing the physical-metaphysical descent of the human soul into matter as a moral failure accompanied by moral guilt. I saw and still see that a shadow lies over the human story, but I could not see that this should be stated in terms of the catechism affirmation that all human beings are conceived and born children of wrath.

III

What Pelagius stood for most of all was human freedom and responsibility and with that the goodness of creation and of man/woman as the image of God. This was accompanied by a strong asceticism and a strong sense of personal sin as leading to punishment and involving what seem to us extreme personal penances such as later culminated in the Irish Penitentials. Thus Pelagianism became a kind of elitism or puritanism, and in this matter Augustine seems more sensitive to human needs and to the pathos of the two laws of St. Paul (Rom. 7.22–23). Pelagius tended to see things in black and white and to say that if man is seen as too weak to obey the law of God then there is no freedom and therefore no sin.

Pelagius belongs to a strong ascetical tradition that tends to take literally the 'hard sayings' of the gospel, though he pays lip-service to the distinction between precepts which must be obeyed and counsels which are only for the perfect. Pelagius the monk was interested only in the perfect and was, it seems, a man of admitted sanctity of life; Augustine the bishop was equally concerned with the weaker members of his flock and their desperate dependence on divine help. Yet Augustine tended to fall into an elitism of predestination according to which some are chosen by God and some, perhaps the majority, are rejected. He made our destiny depend on an arbitrary divine decree which could not be questioned and looked very much like tyranny. This was taken over by Calvin in the Reform theology of the double decree, satirised only too tellingly by Robert Burns in 'Holy Willie's Prayer':

> O Thou, wha in the heavens dost dwell,
> Wha, as it pleases best thysel',
> Sends ane to heaven and ten to hell,
> A' for thy glory,
> And no for ony guid or ill
> They've done afore thee!

Against this kind of theology, now generally rejected except by extreme Protestant fundamentalists, Pelagius and Pelagianism stand firm. It cannot, however, be said that Catholic theology goes the way of Pelagius and succeeds in avoiding predestination; indeed, one can see how Calvin came to say that St. Thomas Aquinas would have had to accept predestination and double decree had he been consistent. It seems indeed that Aquinas for part of his life was close to Pelagius and was forced to pull away from him when he discovered the full amplitude of the condemnation of Pelagianism in its semi-Pelagian form.[34] The shadow of the condemnations of Pelagius lies heavy on all the Christian churches, both Catholic and Protestant. I shall look more fully at this in the next section, which has to do with the

[34] See Peter Brown, *Augustine of Hippo* (London: Faber & Faber, 1985), ch. 33.

concept of heresy in the Christian tradition and the possibility of getting beyond it.

IV

It is well to begin by making a three-way distinction between (a) the Pelagian heresy, (b) the Pelagian temper of mind, and (c) Pelagian theology. I shall take these three complex phenomena in reverse order, so that by putting two of them on one side we may concentrate on the third, though indeed all three are historically and practically important.

Pelagian theology, as we have seen, strongly emphasises the reality of human freedom and human responsibility. It seems to stand in opposition to St. Augustine's emphasis on divine grace and man's absolute need for the divine presence and divine help in every single action and thought that unites him to God. Without the inner mysterious action of grace, natural man can only do evil when he appears to be doing good and following a high ethical code of conduct. Pelagian theology does not reject the presence of and the need for God's grace. Grace, *gratia*, is simply the Latin for 'gift freely given', and Pelagius sees creation itself as the greatest of all such gifts, accompanied by the further gifts of God's continuing care of his own creation, which in the Genesis account of creation God saw was good, indeed very good (Gen. 1.31). Pelagian theology makes much of the Old Testament, of the goodness of creation and of the *imago dei* text, Gen. 1.27, according to which God made man and woman 'according to his own image and likeness', a text which is the true charter of woman's rights and dignity from the beginning. In all this, according to Pelagian theology, divine grace is present and operative and is named by a modern commentator on Pelagius *Gratia* IA (creation) and *Gratia* IB (the divine care of creation). Beyond and continuous with this grace is the grace of the old (Mosaic) law (*Gratia* IIA) which is fulfilled and completed by the new law of Christ (*Gratia* IIB) and which shone forth in the faith of Abraham (*Gratia* IIIA), and as the grace of Christ shines forth in the fullest splendour of divine giving in Christian baptism with its threefold presence of sacrament, desire and martyrdom (*Gratia* IIIB).[35]

Here is a very rich theology of grace, but it is a theology of continuity in which nature is continuous with the supernatural, whereas the theology of Augustine which has tended to dominate Western Christianity, especially in its Reform theologies, is a theology of discontinuity in which all natural ethics and natural goodness are totally blighted by the deadly virus of original sin. For Pelagian theology, which has had various reincarnations within both Catholic and Reform theology and is being trumpeted loudly and rather naively in some contemporary theologies of creation, this deadly virus is at most a shadow that falls across the human story but does not at all infect or destroy the goodness of creation and of natural man and woman.

V

Closely related to this theology yet nevertheless distinct from it is the *Pelagian temper* or attitude of mind which has been a constant presence in Celtic Christianity from the earliest times and involves a special attitude to created nature in human beings themselves and in the natural world of the kingdoms of nature: mineral, plant, animal and 'spirit'. This attitude is all-pervasive in the myths, traditions and prayers of the peoples of the Celtic fringe (Irish, Scottish, Welsh, Breton, Basque, etc.) and the Celtic survival (in France and Germany, etc.), but it can best be seen in its original and continuing freshness and strangeness in the eighth-century *Lorica Sti Patritii* or 'Breastplate' of St Patrick

[35] See T. Bohlin, *Die Theologie des Pelagius und ihre Genesis* (Uppsala: Lundequistska Bokhandeln, 1957).

(to whom it came to be attributed). Scholars have tended to lump it together with other *Loricae* or protection prayers of the period as an amalgam of Christian and pre-Christian religious attitudes. This is a way of killing it off and putting it in a glass-case in a museum, where scholars can wrangle over dead words, but many people have responded in modern times to its freshness and its frank acceptance of creation. Thus the Pelagian temper lives on even among those who would not want to accept the Pelagian theology, about which they know little or nothing, and who would be horrified at the idea of their being tainted by the Pelagian, or any other, type of heresy.

What then is the Pelagian heresy? To try to answer this it is necessary to look at what French scholarship in recent times has come to name *Hérésiologie*, heresiology.

VI

Hilaire Belloc, who tended to see things clearly in black and white, summed up the Pelagian heresy by saying, in a drinking song aimed at all heretics by jolly, hard-drinking true believers, that Pelagius

> Did not believe in Adam and Eve
> And laughed at original sin.

This is very much a false simplification, false largely because it *is* a simplification. Yet there is a certain justice in the fact that Pelagius has had to suffer the fate of being simplified into heresy, for he himself came as a great simplifier from the Isles of the North to Rome, as a breath of cold fresh air into a city then as now overheated with the ambiguities of sophisticated self-interest parading as orthodox Christianity. To quote Peter Brown, 'The conventional "good man" of pagan Rome had quite unthinkingly become the conventional "good Christian" of the fifth century.' 'Such a man', adds Peter Brown, 'was capable of discussing at the dinner table both the latest theological opinion and the kind of judicial torture he had just inflicted on some poor wretch.'[36] Pelagius broke into this comfortable Christianity like a bolt from the blue, like a cold blast from the north, preaching human freedom and human responsibility and saying that the grace of God was no substitute for this freedom and this responsibility. Augustine felt that this bleak emphasis on man's freedom could only lead finally to the denial of the grace of God as utterly gratuitous and in no way dependent on man's initiative. This ascetical libertarian approach, Augustine says, leads straight to the denial of God's grace. And so Peter Brown, a writer most sympathetic to Augustine, is led to say, 'Pelagian*ism* as we know it, that consistent body of ideas of momentous consequences, had come into existence; but in the mind of Augustine, not of Pelagius.'[37]

However, Peter Brown adds a paragraph which can make one think again in dealing with the age-old problem of Augustine versus Pelagius.

> The basic difference between the two men, however, is to be found in two radically different views on the relation between man and God. It is summed up succinctly in their choice of language. Augustine had long been fascinated by babies: the extent of their helplessness had grown upon him even since he wrote the *Confessions*, and in the *Confessions* he had had no hesitation in likening his relation to God to that of a baby to its mother's breast, utterly dependent, intimately involved in all the good and evil that might come from this, the only source of life.
>
> The Pelagian, by contrast, was contemptuous of babies. 'There is no more pressing admonition than this, that we should be called *sons* of God.' To be a 'son' was to become an entirely separate person, no longer dependent on one's

[36] Brown, *Augustine of Hippo*, pp. 346, 347.
[37] Brown, *Augustine of Hippo*, p. 345.

> father, but capable of following out by one's own power, the good deeds that he had commanded. The Pelagian was *emancipatus a deo*; it is a brilliant image taken from the language of Roman family law: freed from the all-embracing and claustrophobic rights of the father of a great family over his children, these sons had 'come of age'. They had been 'released', as in Roman Law, from dependence on the *pater familias* and could at last go out into the world as mature, free individuals, able to uphold in heroic deeds the good name of their illustrious ancestry: '*Be ye perfect, even as Your Father in Heaven is perfect.*'[38]

VII

In his article on Pelagianism in the *Dictionnaire de Spiritualité*, the celebrated scholar Aimé Solignac talks of 'heresiology' as a literary genre which tends to distort the ideas of so-called 'heretics', first by discovering links between their writings and well-known heretics from the past, and secondly by reducing the whole system of the 'heretics' to a series of 'theses' baldly stated without the least nuance or explanation. This has been used all through Christian history and Pelagius especially has been the victim of it. Where Pelagius, and with him the whole Celtic tradition in one of its aspects, is open to criticism – leaving aside the word 'heresy' as unhelpful and exaggerative – is in his extreme asceticism which led on to the medieval Irish Penitentials.

Finally, we are left with two questions: first, that of the usefulness and limits of the concept of heresy, and secondly, that of the possibility of finding some guidance and helpfulness in the theology and temper of mind of Pelagius and Pelagianism.

38 Brown, *Augustine of Hippo*, pp. 351–2.

As regards heresy it is difficult to avoid the need for some check on those who set themselves up as teachers of truth within a certain tradition. Yet it can be argued that this is not best met by way of the concept of heresy so much as by way of free and open discussion, in other words by way of what has traditionally been one of the main functions of academics and universities, as well as by a healthy climate of open discussion. (In our own day this essential function of universities is being put in jeopardy by underfunding and that vocationalism which is only concerned with turning out professionals, clergymen and teachers of religion among others.)

As regards the theology of Pelagius, I would link it up with the general approach to nature and creation in Celtic Christianity. Jesus Christ, true man and true God, came not only into that Greek philosophy which could describe, if not define, him as *logos* and divine-human *hypostasis*; not only into that Roman world which could by its laws and its roads carry the good news to the ends of the empire. He also came in the flesh and in that vitality that is common to all that lives and dies, came as part of that *natura* that is indeed corruptible but contains within it, somehow – Augustine cannot tell us, though he wrestles long and hard with the problem – something incorruptible yet at the same time physical and material: what the ancients call *materia caelestis*, heavenly matter. Man's fall from grace, however one understands it, is indeed all around us in this corruptible world, yet this leaves the human being free, with the help of original grace, to reach towards the incorruptible within himself and beyond himself.